HISTORIC MACON
An Illustrated History
by James Barfield

Commissioned by the Historic Macon Foundation

Historical Publishing Network
A division of Lammert Incorporated
San Antonio, Texas

Confederate Monument, Court House and Opera House, Macon, Ga.

First Edition

Copyright © 2007 Historical Publishing Network

All rights reserved. No part of this book may be reproduced in any form or by any means, electronic or mechanical, including photocopying, without permission in writing from the publisher. All inquiries should be addressed to Historical Publishing Network, 11555 Galm Road, Suite 100, San Antonio, Texas, 78254. Phone (800) 749-9790.

ISBN: 9781893619791
Library of Congress Card Catalog Number: 2007940524

Historic Macon: An Illustrated History

author:	James Barfield
cover artist:	George Beattle
contributing writer for "Sharing the Heritage":	Britt Fayssoux
	Brenda Thompson

Historical Publishing Network

president:	Ron Lammert
project managers:	David H. White
	Ray Perry
administration:	Donna M. Mata
	Evelyn Hart
	Melissa Quinn
book sales:	Dee Steidle
production:	Colin Hart
	Craig Mitchell
	Charles A. Newton III

Contents

4	Preface	
5	Chapter I	*sacred settlement*
8	Chapter II	*cotton town*
23	Chapter III	*war center*
33	Chapter IV	*town of the new South*
47	Chapter V	*twentieth century city*
57	Chapter VI	*into the new millennium*
62	Bibliography	
64	Sharing the Heritage	
106	Sponsors	
107	About the Author	
107	About the Cover	

❖

Opposite: An artist's rendering of the courthouse, opera house and Confederate Monument on Mulberry Street.

Below: Mulberry Street as it appears today.

PREFACE

While local history is a subject often overlooked by schools it is one that citizens seem to enjoy and want to know about. It is essential for an understanding of a place and its development. This history is meant to provide some understanding of Macon and how it came to be the city that it is. To cover Macon's history in depth would require several large volumes. This history is a compact synthesis compiled from many sources which were produced through many years. All local historians owe a huge debt to John. C. Butler and his 1879 history of early Macon. Similarly, Macon's newspapers provide an indispensable source of information. In 1949 Julius Gholson, Clara Nell Hargrove and Ida Young collaborated on a valuable history of the city to that date. In 1979 Nancy Briska Anderson wrote an excellent history with appropriate illustrations for *The Macon Telegraph* and *The Macon News*. In 1989 Kristina Simms produced a similarly fine history for the Middle Georgia Historical Society. The works of these earlier historians provided models as well as facts for this publication.

A vital part of the mission of the Historic Macon Foundation is the preservation of local history. While attention is often focused on the foundation's success in preserving the built environment, staff and members also strive to protect Macon's heritage in other forms. The foundation owns and adds to the Middle Georgia Archives housed at the Washington Memorial Library. It provides presentations on local history for schools and interested groups and operates the Sidney Lanier Cottage as a house museum. It presents regular lectures on history and records oral histories from local residents. It is a natural connection for the Historic Macon Foundation to sponsor this book of Macon history.

The staff of the Genealogical and Historical Room of the Washington Memorial Library constitutes a community asset to be treasured. Especially, Muriel Jackson, Dr. Christopher Stokes, Willard Rocker and Christopher Osier are invaluable to researchers. Gratitude is also owed to Tena Roberts and Sybil McNeil at Wesleyan's library. The photographic talents of Walter Elliott and the technological savvy of James H. Webb aided greatly in the production of this history. Local institutions and business organizations who participated in the publication are to be congratulated for supporting the preservation of Macon's history and the Historic Macon Foundation.

Although historians may strive to achieve accuracy history is a compilation of accounts, many of which tend to disagree with one another. Inaccuracies in this work are unintended, naturally, and regretted sincerely.

Chapter 1

Sacred Settlement

The place now called Macon was home to people a very long time ago. More than ten thousand years ago people lived here who left articles which are their only history. Nature made Macon's location a good place for people to settle. Macon is on the fall line, the place where the mostly flat land of the coastal plain meets the hills of the piedmont. The coastal plain was once under water and where Macon is now was once the shoreline.

In the distant past, long before humans came, the water receded. Remains of a "toothed whale" found near Macon tell of that ancient time. When people came, the water they found here was a river. At the point where the river crosses the fall line there were waterfalls. Probably because of the rushing water at these falls, one group who settled here called the river Ocmulgee which means "bubbling waters".

Early people who settled this area made paths along the fall line from river to river. Augusta on the Savannah River and Columbus on the Chattahoochee are fall line cities once connected by the ancient paths. The fall line location was always important because travel on the rivers always stopped at the waterfalls.

Little is known about the first people to settle on the fall line at the Ocmulgee. Some experts believe they came from what is now Mexico. They used tools made of flint which were similar to designs used in Mexico. They did no farming, but got their food by hunting and fishing. These people left no record of what they called themselves. Columbus called the people he encountered in this part of the world Indians, and that name came to mean all the native people of America.

Mounds built by prehistoric settlers at the Ocmulgee Old Fields are now protected as part of the Ocmulgee National Monument.

The first Indians to settle at the fall line on the Ocmulgee disappeared almost eight thousand years before Christ. The group who settled there next was known as the "Shell Fish Eaters" because they ate many oysters and clams which were to be found then in the Ocmulgee. The shells and pottery they left tell us about their lives. They were in the area between five and one thousand years before Christ.

A third group that settled in the area was called the Early Farmers. They grew tobacco, beans and pumpkins. About 900 A.D. these people also disappeared and were replaced by the Master Farmers who had advanced farming methods and who built solid houses and temples. Some time after 1350 A.D., a group called the Reconquest People took control of the river valley. They seem to have been a mixture of the Master Farmers and new tribes who moved into the area.

An early twentieth century artist's sketch of Fort Benjamin Hawkins based on remnants remaining at the fort site and on contemporary descriptions.

None of the Indian groups who lived on the Ocmulgee had writing, so they were prehistoric. Macon's written history began in 1540 when the Spanish explorer, Hernando de Soto, visited the Reconquest People at their village on the Ocmulgee. Indians told him tales of gold always farther away. No doubt, they were hoping to get rid of the strange foreigner who demanded so much from them.

Priests who traveled with de Soto kept diaries. An event described in one of the diaries took place at an important village above the point where the Ocmulgee and Oconee Rivers meet to form the Altamaha River. That village almost certainly was the Ocmulgee Old Fields at the present site of Macon. An Indian guide traveling with de Soto was injured and dying. The priest urged him to accept the Christian religion and he was baptized with Ocmulgee River water. That was the fist baptism recorded in American history.

De Soto moved on, searching for gold he never found. Other Spaniards and, later, Englishmen came to the Ocmulgee Old Fields to trade with the Indians they called "Hitchiti" or Creeks. The foreign traders were impressed by the huge earth mounds the Indians had made. Using rough tools and baskets the Indians built the mounds for several uses. Some mounds were for burying the dead. Others were foundations for wooden buildings used as places to worship the gods or observe the heavens. At least one mound was hollow and used as a special meeting place for leaders of the village.

In 1733 William Bartram, an English scientist who studied plants, visited Ocmulgee Old Fields and described the "magnificent ruins" he saw there. That same year General James Oglethorpe founded the colony of Georgia. In 1739 he visited the village on the Ocmulgee. Indians throughout the area began to trade with the English, and the Ocmulgee settlement became a major trading center. Indians in Florida who were loyal to Spain were captured by the English, enslaved, and taken to South Carolina. Ocmulgee Old Fields was the main stopping point on the slave route.

For some time after Americans won their independence from England, the Ocmulgees held their village and the Creeks controlled middle Georgia. But the Indians' control of their ancestral homeland was threatened by the Americans' hunger for land. In 1797 President George Washington appointed his friend Benjamin Hawkins Indian agent for western Georgia. Hawkins reported to the government that the Ocmulgee Valley offered fine water, timber and soil.

In 1806 the government set up a trading post on top of the highest hill near the Ocmulgee Old Fields village. It was named Fort Benjamin Hawkins and was designed for defense. The 14-acre post was enclosed by a wall of logs 14 feet high. Two main buildings called blockhouses were built at opposite ends of the post. There were 28 feet square and 34 feet high, with stone walls for the first floors and log walls above. Small gaps were left in the walls through which guns could be fired if Indians attacked.

Relations between people living at Fort Hawkins and their Indian neighbors were not always friendly, but no records told of fighting at the fort. During the War of 1812 troops were gathered at the fort on the way to fight elsewhere. Captain Phillip Cook was the fort's commander. In 1813 his daughter, Martha, was the first white child born in the area.

General Andrew Jackson, Indian fighter and hero of the War of 1812, camped near Fort Hawkins in 1818. He was on his way to fight Indians in Florida. The place where he is believed to have camped became known as Jackson Springs and is today a city park.

A store and an inn were built outside the fort's walls in 1819, and the next year, a growing settlement there was named Newtown. Two of the settlers started a flatboat business to float cotton grown in nearby Jones County down the Ocmulgee and the Altamaha to the coast. As the number of settlers at Newtown grew, so did their demands that the government push out the Indians and open for settlement the land west of the river. At Indian Springs in 1821, twenty-six Creek chiefs signed a treaty giving the United States Government all land between the Ocmulgee and the Flint River to the west. Included as well were the sacred village and land around it called the Ocmulgee Old Fields. Most of the Indians moved west, leaving not more than one hundred of their tribe to remain at the home of their ancestors.

From what had been the Indians' land, the Georgia General Assembly created four new counties in December 1822. The county that included Fort Hawkins and Newtown was named for Dr. William Wyatt Bibb who had recently died. A Virginia native, Dr. Bibb had been a United States congressman and senator from Georgia and the first governor of Alabama.

Two weeks after Bibb County was created, the General Assembly appointed five commissioners to plan a county seat, a town to be called Macon. The name honored Nathaniel Macon of North Carolina who served in Congress for thirty-seven years. Thomas Jefferson called Macon "the last of the Romans" and John Randolph said he was "the wisest man I ever knew". Senator Macon had relatives who settled in Macon and he was believed to have visited the town named for him.

James Webb, a surveyor and engineer, was chosen to survey a site for the new town to be built on the west bank of the Ocmulgee across from the old Indian village. The surveyor and five commissioners drew a plan of rectangles divided into smaller rectangles. Wide streets formed blocks divided by lanes into smaller blocks. Streets running parallel to the river were named for trees, those perpendicular to the river were numbered. Open spaces between blocks were set aside for a courthouse square, a public market, a cemetery, and a village school. Lots were set aside for use by the Episcopal, Methodist, Baptist, and Presbyterian Churches.

At the time the plan was drawn, no building stood inside the boundaries of the planned town. In March 1823 lots were offered for sale. Immediately, Macon pioneer settlers moved in and began to clear their lots, build their houses and make the planned town a real one.

The original building constructed as Bibb County's courthouse in 1828 was a handsome structure located on the original courthouse square at Fifth and Mulberry Streets.

Chapter II

Cotton Town

This 1880 view of steam engines of the Central of Georgia Railroad illustrates Macon's role as a hub of a large rail network and center of train transportation since the 1840s.

From its beginning the newly created town of Macon was a success. In spite of fires, floods, and financial crises, the town grew for almost forty years. Macon succeeded for many reasons, but three of the most important ones were location, leadership and cotton. The great profits to be made in shipping cotton made Macon a place of opportunity. Its location on a river at the fall line which had made it a center of Indian travel also made it a crossroads for the cotton trade. The opportunity Macon offered attracted outstanding people who led it to succeed.

On a Georgia plantation in 1793, Eli Whitney invented a simple way to remove cotton seeds from the valuable fiber. This meant that England's rich cotton industry could get more cotton from planters in the American South and the planters could make large profits. Macon lay in the center of Georgia's cotton-growing area and at the head of traffic on a river connecting cotton farms and the coast. Other Georgia towns became cotton markets and shipping points, but Macon also had smart, hard-working leaders who kept it ahead of its competition.

Records of early Macon included the names of people who helped the young town grow. Names of certain leaders appeared often, connected with many activities. By their efforts these early leaders earned the title "City Fathers."

Simri Rose was a young man when he helped create Macon. As an old man he often said that Macon was his "first child." Rose was nineteen in 1818 when he arrived at the Newtown settlement.

Above: Macon's original entry from the east was via the Fifth Street bridge. Several bridges were destroyed by floods in the Nineteenth Century. Today the bridge at this site is named for native son Otis Redding and Fifth Street is now Dr. Martin Luther King, Jr., Boulevard.

Left: Simri Rose as much as anyone deserves the title "Father of Macon." His newspaper, The Georgia Messenger, provided a record of early Macon history. His civic contributions were manifold and, more than anyone, he worked to make Macon a beautiful town.

Born and educated in Connecticut, he came to Newtown from New York where he had written for *Harper's Magazine*. In the frontier settlement he wrote for a newspaper called *The Bulldog*. When it crossed the Ocmulgee to become Macon's first newspaper, its name became *The Georgia Messenger*. Rose bought a partnership in the paper and was its editor for almost fifty years.

Rose helped create the plan for Macon. He insisted that major streets be 180 feet wide, alternating streets be 120 feet wide. His idea was to limit crowding, fire, and disease. Rose also made the streets of Macon shady. Throughout his life when he saw a spot he felt needed a tree, he took servant, horse and buggy to the Ocmulgee swamps, found the right tree, and transplanted it to the empty spot.

Rose's house on Beall's Hill overlooking Macon was set on four acres crowded with all kinds of trees, shrubs, flowers and plants. He received seeds and cuttings from all over the world. He began the Central Horticultural Society and often won prizes in its plant shows.

Rose's love of plants led to the achievement for which he was to be remembered most, Rose Hill Cemetery. In 1838 he headed a committee to find a site

Chapter II ◆ 9

Above: Washington Poe, attorney, judge, and early mayor of Macon, was often a force for calm and reason in the young town.

Right: Ambrose Baber was a pioneer Macon physician who led the effort to create Christ Church Episcopal and who contributed to many civic improvements. His library formed the basis of Macon's first lending library.

for a new city burial ground. They chose a place a mile and a half above the town on a high bluff overlooking the river. Rose managed the clearing and planting of the new site and was rewarded by a resolution of the city council on March 27, 1840. He was given his choice of a lot in the new cemetery and it was named Rose Hill in his honor.

Simri Rose worked on many projects in young Macon. He organized the Episcopal Sunday School and was a vestryman of Christ Church. He held high offices in the Freemasons Society and was an original member of Macon's first military corps, The Macon Volunteers. He was a trustee of Macon's first school, the Bibb County Academy, and an original supporter when the Georgia Academy for the Blind was located in Macon. The Volunteer Fire Department honored his long service to it by naming an engine "The Simri Rose." When Rose died in 1869 his newspaper wrote of him, "No man ever lived in Macon who showed more public spirit and unselfish interest in her welfare."

When Simri Rose had been at Newtown two years another man arrived who also played a major role in the founding of Macon. He, too, was from Connecticut and had been a newspaperman. His name was Oliver Hillhouse Prince. In 1796, at age fourteen, Prince moved Washington, Georgia to help his aunt run a newspaper. In 1806 he became a lawyer. He was elected to the Georgia Legislature and, in 1822, was appointed to the commission to create Macon. When lots were sold in the new town, he bought one at the corner of Plum and Fifth Streets. On his lot he built a combination house and law office. There he lived, worked, and served as one of the five commissioners who governed Macon.

Prince was a leader in improving the new town. He helped set up the Bibb County Academy and became a director of Macon's first bank. In 1828 he was appointed to a vacant seat in Congress. In 1831 Prince presided at a convention to discuss building a railroad from Savannah to Macon. His name was familiar to all Georgia lawyers because he had put together the first digest of the state's laws.

Prince's wife and family remained in Macon after he bought, in 1832, a newspaper in Milledgeville, the state capital, and moved there to run it. After three years Prince sold the

newspaper and moved with his wife and family to Athens. The next year he and his wife, Mary, were drowned in a steamship wreck. Their bodies were brought to Macon and buried in Rose Hill Cemetery.

One of the great favors Oliver Hillhouse Prince did for Macon was bringing his friend, Dr. Ambrose Baber, to the town as an original settler. A native of Virginia, Dr. Baber studied medicine at the Medical College of Philadelphia. He was nineteen when he joined the army in the War of 1812. He was seriously wounded, but volunteered again in 1817 to serve as surgeon with Andrew Jackson fighting Indians in Florida. He then settled in Twiggs County, Georgia, until 1823 when he moved to Macon. Although his war wound never healed properly and he suffered from severe asthma, Dr. Baber did as much as anyone for his new hometown.

In 1825, Dr. Baber served as Worshipful Master of the Freemasons Society. That organization arranged for a visit to Macon by the Revolutionary War hero, the Marquis de Lafayette. Dr. Baber had the honor of giving the speech of welcome to the famous visitor. His moment of honor was followed by a period of scandal. In a duel he shot and killed the State Prosecutor of Georgia. In the South in the 1820s, duels were illegal, but men still fought them to settle questions of honor.

The scandal did not prevent Ambrose Baber's being elected to the State Senate for four terms. As a senator he saved the woods south of Macon from being cut for firewood. The land was made a reserve and later became Central City Park. In the legislature, Dr. Baber worked for canals, railroads and public education in Georgia.

In 1829, Ambrose Baber married a Savannah girl, Mary Elizabeth Sweet, and built for her a

Above: Elam Alexander was a "master builder", or architect, by profession but also a very successful businessman responsible for bringing the telegraph to Macon. His endowment of a fund for public education still serves the community today.

Left: Wesleyan College, originally Georgia Female College, is the oldest college in the world chartered to grant degrees to women. Originally housed in the Greek Revival building atop Encampment Hill, now College Hill, the school has a long and distinguished history of educating women.

Right: In the Nineteenth Century train passengers used several stations. The Union Depot, now demolished, was one.

Below: In 1879 Wesleyan updated its building with a fashionable Victorian façade. This building's destruction by fire in 1963 remains Macon's most significant architectural loss.

Opposite, top: "The Palace on the Hill" was the local designation for entrepreneur Jerry Cowles' Greek Revival mansion built between 1836 and 1840. Designed by Elam Alexander, the house in 1865 served as Union General Wilson's residence during the occupation of Macon by Federal forces. Now called "Woodruff House", it belongs to Mercer University.

Opposite, bottom: By 1842 eight regular steamboats traveled between Macon and Darien on the coast. Construction of railroads combined with silting of the river made steamboat traffic less attractive and it ended in 1930.

house on Walnut Street. It was described as "By far the handsomest building in town." In it he placed his library of more than twelve hundred books in seven languages.

The same year he built his house, Dr. Baber traveled to Boston where he first saw a railroad. Excited by this new form of transportation he returned to Georgia to work for a railroad to connect Macon to Savannah. It 1833 he helped obtain from the Legislature a charter for the Central of Georgia Line and, in 1835, a large grant of money to develop the railroad. On his return from the state capital he was honored with a torchlight parade through Macon's streets.

Ambrose Baber was president of Macon's first bank and, later, Macon agent for the Bank of the United States. In the election of 1840 he supported the Whig Party. When the Whigs won he was rewarded with an appointment as United States Representative to the Kingdom of Sardinia. He went to Milan, Italy, and served there for four years.

❖

Above: The City of Macon *carried passengers and freight the two hundred miles down the Ocmulgee and Altamaha Rivers.*

Right: Sidney Lanier was born in Macon in 1842. Best known during his lifetime for his musical compositions, he became celebrated for his poetry after his early death at age 39. "Corn", "The Marshes of Glynn", and "The Song of the Chattahoochee" are three of his best known works. He served as a scout in General Robert E. Lee's army but was captured and interned at a prison camp in Maryland. At war's end he walked most of the way back to Macon.

In 1846, Dr. Baber again ran for the State Senate. A false rumor that he led a mob that "tarred, feathered, and ran out of town" a democrat cost him the election by a few votes. After his loss, Dr. Baber was a pitiful figure. He suffered from his war wound, severe asthma and increasing

curvature of the spine. In that condition he prescribed medicine for a patient. On the advice of a pharmacist the patient refused to take the medicine Dr. Baber prescribed. To prove his prescription was correct the doctor took two teaspoons of the medicine with a lump of sugar. Before he could loosen his collar Dr. Baber was dead. An investigation revealed a printing error in the prescription book.

Newspapers printing the story of Dr. Baber's death noted the many things he had done for Macon. He was a major supporter of Montpelier Institute, a girls' school just west of Macon. He was the first president of the Macon Lyceum and Literary Society and his books were the basis of that lending library. Christ Episcopal Church preserved the silver communion service he gave it, and it was noted that "Christ Church owes more to him than any other man." The Masons placed a marble monument at his grave in Rose Hill Cemetery. A fellow doctor who had known him said of Ambrose Baber, "He was deeply interested in the prosperity of the young place in which he had settled, and was ranked among its most enterprising and public-spirited citizens."

Another most enterprising and public-spirited early citizen of Macon was Edward Dorr Tracy. He was born in Connecticut in 1791, went to public schools there, and then worked in a shipping business in New York City. In 1818 he started the study of law. In June 1824 the Macon newspaper carried a notice that Edward D. Tracy would practice law as partner of Oliver Hillhouse Prince. Tracy quickly became an active citizen of the young town. He was an original member of the Macon Bar, a member of the first vestry of Christ Church, a trustee of the Bibb County Academy, and Junior Warden of the Masonic Lodge. At a town celebration on July 4, 1825, Tracy read the Declaration of Independence.

At the most exciting event of Macon's early history, the visit of Lafayette, Tracy made the toast. He was able to speak to Lafayette in French, Spanish, and American Indian. The Frenchman noted that Tracy was the only American he had met who could speak to him in the native American language.

In 1826, Edward D. Tracy became Intendant of Macon, a position much the same as mayor. City records listed Tracy as Macon's first mayor because the two previous intendants were appointed rather than elected.

In 1828, Tracy married Susan Campbell. She died in 1834 and Tracy married her sister, Caroline. Their house was on Georgia Avenue. In the 1850s it was replaced by a new house for his daughter, Ann Tracy Johnston. That house, a mansion of Italianate design, became a Macon landmark known as the Johnston-Hay House.

In 1836, Tracy was a delegate to a Knoxville, Tennessee, railroad convention at which he helped to arrange for a rail line to come from Tennessee through Macon. In 1838 he was elected to the Georgia General Assembly. In 1841 he became Judge of Superior Court. The judge who followed Tracy in that position overturned nineteen of his decisions, but the Georgia Supreme Court upheld Judge Tracy's decision in every case.

Tracy returned to his private law practice in 1845 and was a leading business lawyer until his death in 1849. On the day of his funeral in Rose Hill Cemetery, the Macon Bar passed a resolution that called Judge Tracy "A gentleman of warm heart and refined feelings, the chosen friend of his Constituency, the upright and profound Judge."

A native Georgian who became a pioneer Macon lawyer and early intendant was Washington Poe. Born in Augusta in 1799, Poe was educated in New Jersey and Connecticut before he settled in Macon in 1825. By the next

This house was built for Dr. Ambrose Baber in 1829 and after his death became the home of John Basil Lamar. Called "The Bear's Den", it often was occupied by Lamar's sister, Mary Ann, and her husband, Howell Cobb, during the war. At her brother's death in battle Mrs. Cobb inherited the house. Renovated to house a medical clinic in the 1920s, the structure now houses law offices.

Augustus O. Bacon was a Macon attorney who served twenty-five years in the state legislature and eighteen years in the United States Senate. His bequest of his estate, Baconsfield, to the City of Macon for use as a park for "white women and children" was challenged in court under the Civil Rights Act of 1964 and the Supreme Court of the United States ruled that the property be returned to his heirs. This decision cost Macon one of its most valued community assets.

year he was an important citizen. He was chosen to give a memorial speech at the court house after Thomas Jefferson and John Adams both died on the Fourth of July—the fiftieth anniversary of the signing of the Declaration of Independence. That same year he founded Macon's first Bible society. He tried Macon's first murder case and helped organize its first school. In 1827 he followed Edward D. Tracy as Macon Intendant.

On Christmas Eve, 1829, Poe married Selina Norman, who was the sister of Mrs. Oliver Hillhouse Prince. When the Princes were drowned, Poe became guardian of the three Prince children. Another family connection was Edgar Allen Poe, one of the South's finest authors. In 1840 Edgar Allen Poe wrote his Macon cousin asking for help in starting a magazine. Washington Poe's response was not recorded.

In 1831 Poe became Solicitor-General for the Flint River Circuit. In that position he became famous for his courage. He ignored many people who threatened his life. When the sheriff was afraid to arrest dangerous law breakers Poe went with him. Poe never carried a weapon, but used the force of his personality to prevent violence. In the election of 1840 a rioting mob broke into the court house and destroyed the ballot box. Poe spoke to the crowd and calmed them, then took the leaders to jail.

In 1844 Poe was elected to Congress, but he had not sought the job and resigned before taking office. In the election of 1860 Poe urged Macon people to remain calm and stay in the Union. He was chosen a delegate to Georgia's secession convention and, with regret, gave his support to the new Confederate Government. During the War Between the States he served as Macon's Postmaster.

The aging lawyer lost most of his fortune in the war and his last years were hard ones. At the death of his son in 1876 Poe seemed to lose the will to live. He died on the day of his son's funeral. After his death a Macon Bar resolution stated, "There is no person among the living or dead who has been so long and so prominently identified with the history of our city."

Not quite as long a resident of Macon but as important in its history as Washington Poe was Elam Alexander. He was Macon's first real architect, he brought the telegraph to town, and he left a fund for education which has benefited generations of young people in Macon.

Elam Alexander was born on a North Carolina farm in 1796. He was able to go to school for only two years. In 1820 he moved to Augusta, Georgia, then to Milledgeville, and, in 1826, to Macon. His occupation was recorded as mechanic.

The first Macon record of Alexander was in 1828 as one of three men hired to build a new court house. The building was constructed in the center of the intersection of Fifth and Mulberry Streets. It was a brick building three stories high with two columned porches and a cupola, or observation room, on the roof. It was described as "The handsomest county edifice in the state." As the court house was being built, Alexander was working on a new building for the Presbyterian Church. In that church in 1838

Central City Park has long been the site for the annual Georgia State Fair. At various times it has seen such uses as a championship horse racing track, an early airfield and a baseball stadium. Its heyday may have come in 1871 when pools, fountains, exhibition halls, a bandstand and elaborate gates were installed.

Gate to Central City Park, Home of Georgia State Fair, Macon, Ga.

Alexander married Ann G. Stone, a widow with two children.

Between his arrival in Macon and his marriage, Elam Alexander was very busy designing and building for the booming young town. In 1836 he worked on a "mansion house" for Dr. Robert Collins, another mansion for Jerry Cowles, and two houses for James Goddard. His largest project that year was a building for the new Georgia Female College, later called Wesleyan. That building was completed in 1839 at a cost of eighty-five thousand dollars.

Elam Alexander was called master builder rather than architect. His ideas came from plan books, but he added touches that were his own. His buildings shared certain features that became his trademarks. He used the Greek Revival style with its large porches with huge columns. He usually placed decorative railings just above the roofline and rows of carved laurel wreaths just below it. On the roofs of his buildings he often placed cupolas, which allowed hot air to rise through the building and escape, and also allowed people to have a view from the highest point of the building.

Alexander's success in building allowed him to expand into other businesses. In 1840 the Central Georgia Railroad had been completed from Savannah to within fifty miles of Macon when building stalled. Alexander and his partner, Robert Collins, completed the rail line in a matter of months, an achievement that brought them public praise and a bonus from the railroad of twenty-five thousand dollars. Alexander's involvement with railroads increased in 1845 when he was made chairman of a commission to create a railroad to connect Macon with the Gulf of Mexico. His success in that project was rewarded by his appointment as president of the newly formed Southwestern Railroad Company.

In 1847 Elam Alexander secured a telegraph line for Macon. He was in Savannah when plans were being made to extend the Morse Telegraph from Augusta through Atlanta to New Orleans. Alexander put up ten thousand dollars of his own money to have the line brought through Macon instead. He became president of the Macon office of the Washington and New Orleans Telegraph Company.

Central City Park from its inception has been a place where Maconites have gathered to enjoy both manmade and natural beauty.

In 1852 Alexander became president of the Manufacturers' Bank and was a major investor in the new Macon Gas Light Company. In 1857 he headed a company which developed a new rail line from Macon to Brunswick. During the War Between the States Alexander was part of a group that formed the Empire State Iron and Coal Mining Works, an industry to aid the war effort. As president of the company, Alexander hoped to make Macon an industrial center, but the effects of the war ruined the project.

Elam Alexander died unexpectedly in March of 1863 and was buried in Rose Hill Cemetery. At his death the newspaper noted Alexander always regretted his lack of formal education, and that he "gave to no organized charities but gave freely to the needy from his own hand."

After his death Alexander continued to give. His will provided money to create a free school for Macon's poor. In 1865 the value of Alexander's fund was about fifty thousand dollars. By 1870 its value had risen to one hundred thousand dollars. The Alexander Free School opened in the house Alexander built for himself. The school was separate from public schools until early in the Twentieth Century when courts ruled that the Board of Education could act as agent for Alexander's fund. That relationship continues.

Elam Alexander's gift to education and the building he created became his lasting memorials in Macon.

Another early Macon citizen who often joined Alexander in projects to benefit the town was Jerry Cowles. He was born in Connecticut in 1802. At sixteen he ran away from his family's farm and traveled to Eatonton, Georgia. He became a partner in a business selling cotton gins, iron and coal.

In Milledgeville in 1829 Cowles married Sarah Caroline Williams, daughter of Georgia's Lieutenant-Governor. Before he moved his wife and infant daughter to Macon in 1830, Cowles

In the nineteenth century, visitors to Central City Park dressed more formally for outings than modern-day picnickers and concert-goers.

 In 1851 the state established the Georgia Academy for the Blind in Macon. It was originally housed in this building facing Orange Street, and the grounds occupied almost an entire block between that street and College Street. In 1905 the school was relocated to its present location in Vineville.

worked with Elam Alexander to plan a house for his family. It was a Greek Revival cottage that experts called one of the finest small houses in the South.

Cowles' arrival marked the beginning of a period of great activity and success for him and for Macon. He was an original investor in Macon's first insurance company and an original member of its first businessmen's club, The Merchant's Meeting, which was the seed for the Rotary Club. He took part in efforts to bring the Central Railroad to Macon and on to Forsyth. Cowles' dream was to make Macon the center of a vast network of railroads. His efforts toward that goal earned him the title, "irrepressible railroad man of the age."

In 1833, Jerry Cowles and Elam Alexander went to Milledgeville to convince the legislature to grant a charter for a Macon to Savannah rail line. Their success helped Cowles become president of the Central Railroad and Banking Company. In 1835 Cowles was Macon's acting mayor while the elected mayor led the Macon Volunteers in the Seminole War in Florida.

Also in 1835 Cowles started the project of which he said at the end of his life he was most proud. He led a committee which convinced the city council to grant five acres of land on Encampment Hill for a female college. He led the drive to raise money for the school with a pledge of one thousand dollars. The Georgia Methodist Conference agreed to sponsor the school which later became known as Wesleyan College.

Encampment Hill was a reserve owned by the town and used by the Macon Volunteers for training camps. When the college was built lots were sold nearby. Houses built on the hill had the benefits of views and breezes. One of those houses was Jerry Cowles' new home.

In 1835, Cowles sold his cottage and bought fourteen acres atop what came to be called Cowles' Hill. Elam Alexander designed for him an elegant mansion with a colonnade of eighteen columns around three of its sides. When the house was completed in 1840 people in Macon referred to it as "the palace on the hill." It is now owned by Mercer University and called Woodruff House.

As the building of his house began, Cowles set out on horseback with Judge Tracy and two colleagues for Knoxville, Tennessee. Their

purpose was to survey the land and convince the Knoxville Railroad Convention to support construction of a line to Macon. They succeeded. One stop on the rail line that was built was called White Hall, which later became Atlanta.

The depression that spread across the country after the Panic of 1837 had an effect on Macon and on Jerry Cowles. He lost a large part of his fortune and gave up his house on the hill. His losses made his most noble act even more noble. In 1845 the unfinished rail line to Forsyth and Atlanta was sold for unpaid debts. The Charleston and Augusta Railroad planned to buy the line and let it die. Jerry Cowles outbid them and saved the line he helped create. Years later a friend of Cowles wrote, "When he bid he represented no one but Jerry Cowles, with no backers but his genius and pluck."

Cowles started several railroads and rescued one, but he was unable to regain his own fortune. In 1849 he left Macon for New York City. When the War Between the States began Cowles returned to Macon and swore an oath of allegiance to the Confederacy. He started an iron business to help the South, but it did not prosper. After the war he looked for new opportunities, but with little success. His friend wrote that he never lost his sense of humor or his spirit, and that he "always held his head high in Macon."

Cowles died in 1877 while visiting his family in New York. His body was returned to Macon and he was buried high on a ridge in Rose Hill Cemetery. His two outstanding houses remain as his monuments in Macon.

Jerry Cowles was the last of the pioneer leaders who came to Macon in its earliest days. An 1826 map of the town printed by Simri Rose includes names of pioneer settlers such as Lamar, Napier, Holt and Ellis. These and other early families made a rough clearing on the frontier into a thriving center of trade.

Leadership, location, and cotton made Macon an important town by 1860. In 1830 fifty thousand bales of cotton were sold in Macon. (A bale of cotton was equal to about four hundred pounds.) In 1858 almost ninety-seven thousand bales were sold, and one planter, Joseph Bond, sold his crop for one hundred thousand dollars.

As early as 1830 Macon held an agricultural fair where farmers could display their products and compete for prizes. The fair was made an annual event in 1851 and, in 1852, visitors from seven states saw exhibitions of rare birds, tropical plants, and the latest steam engines. For the 1860 fair a ship from Belgium sailed up the Ocmulgee and sold a cargo of European goods. From these beginnings Macon established a long tradition as home to the Georgia State Fair.

In 1874 the Society of Jesus, an arm of the Catholic Church, established Pio Nono College at Vineville, Macon's suburb. The name was changed twenty-five years later to Saint Stanislaus College. In 1921 the large building was destroyed by fire and in the blaze hundreds of books were lost, some dating to the early Renaissance. The college did not reopen and, in 1925, a real estate development called Stanislaus was created on its former campus.

Vineville Avenue, Macon, Ga.

❖

The village of Vineville was located nearly two miles from Macon. Named for the plentiful muscadine vines that grew there it was a semi-rural home for many Macon businessmen who were early commuters. Its avenue was lined with their estates and many of their early houses remain.

The value of farm products in Macon in 1860 was estimated at $1.5 million, the value of manufactured products at almost $1 million. Manufacturing began in Macon soon after the town was settled. The first industries were mills for grinding grain and cutting timber. In 1849 a steam-powered cotton mill called the Macon Cotton Factory was opened by John J. Gresham. Its workers were mostly women who were paid $13 a month. Robert Findlay opened a foundry which produced cotton gins and steam engines. By 1860, eighty-eight manufacturing firms were operating in Macon.

By 1842 eight regular steamboats ran between Macon and the coast. The trip usually took a week. After the Central Railroad reached Macon in 1843 a trip to the coast took only a day. By 1860 Macon had direct trains to Savannah, Atlanta, Tennessee and Southwest Georgia. Lines were being completed to Brunswick and Augusta.

Records from the last year of peace before the War Between the States showed how the town of Macon had grown. Sixty-seven new houses were built. Macon had twenty-seven doctors and the same number of lawyers. It had fifty-seven stores selling food, twenty stores selling dry goods, four book stores, and three slave markets. There were two newspapers, one of them printed daily. Macon had five large hotels, four banks, and two theatres. Concert Hall and Ralston Hall presented concerts, lectures, operas and plays. Schools included the Bibb Academy, The Macon Common School, and several private academies. Thirteen hundred Macon students were taught by thirty-four teachers. Wesleyan Female College and the Botanical and Medical College offered higher education. Churches served six denominations. The population of Bibb County stood at fifteen thousand with about half that number living in the town limits.

Macon grew and developed for almost forty years after it was settled. Sometimes its progress was slowed by depressions, sometimes by fires, floods, and accidents, but progress continued. As the War Between the States began Macon entered the period of its greatest role in American history. That period was also the time of the greatest threat to Macon's survival.

City Hall, Macon, Ga.

Chapter III

War Center

The war that began in 1861 was the result of old differences between the sections of the country. No simple reason made the Southern states secede, declaring independence from the United States. From the country's beginning disagreements about the tariff, states' rights and slavery divided North and South.

The tariff, the national tax on goods imported into the United States, helped Northern manufacturers by making foreign goods more expensive. Southerners, with few factories, resented high tariffs because they imported most of their manufactured goods in trade for cotton. South Carolina threatened to leave the Union in 1833 when a high tariff was passed by Congress. Macon voters that year elected candidates of the Unionist Party and so voted against the idea of secession. But Macon continued to resent the tariff and to fight against it.

When the United States Constitution was written it was opposed by many who believed it took too much power from the states. They believed that independence of the states was the best guarantee that the national government would not become too powerful and take away individual rights. In Macon in the 1830s people who held those beliefs joined the States' Rights Party. Until 1860 that party was not strong in Macon. The leaders, the newspapers, and the majority of voters were loyal to the Union.

A right that Southerners made sure was recognized in the Constitution was that of owning slaves. As cotton became the South's main crop, slaves became more valuable. Slavery meant that human beings could be bought and sold, that families could be split apart by owners, and that slaves were property and had no rights as people. Southerners believed in the Declaration of Independence and the Bill of Rights, but they realized that slaves meant cotton and cotton meant money.

The central portion of Macon's City Hall was built to house a bank. When the bank failed it saw several years' service as a "fireproof" cotton warehouse. The city acquired it in 1860 and, in 1865 it served briefly as Georgia's State Capitol. The only person killed in battle in Macon was a sentry on its porch shot by Federal troops.

Chapter III ✦ 23

Above: Elam Alexander designed this fine Greek Revival house built for Judge Asa Holt in 1853. In 1864 a cannonball fired from across the Ocmulgee by Gen. Stoneman's artillery struck the house. It remained in the Holt family until 1962 when it was acquired by the United Daughters of the Confederacy and opened as a museum. It is furnished with period pieces including two rooms preserved by the Adelphean and Philomathean Societies from the original Wesleyan College building.

In 1860 Bibb County had almost sixty-eight hundred slaves making up forty-two per cent of the population. Only thirty-three slave holders in the county owned more than ten slaves, so most slaves lived on farms or in town rather than on large plantations.

As slaves were valuable property it was to the owners' benefit to take care of them. One Bibb County planter bought his slaves clothes from New York. He signed a contract with a local doctor to give medical care to his slaves and another with his farm manager never to mistreat a slave. During the war he ordered that his slaves must have good shoes "whatever the cost".

Some slaves escaped. Two from Bibb County who did were Ellen and William Craft. She was the daughter of a slave woman and a white lawyer. He was a cabinet maker. Ellen disguised herself as a young gentleman and William posed as "his" slave. Together they escaped to the North. After the war they returned to Georgia and opened a trade school for blacks.

Not all blacks in Bibb County were slaves before the war. The 1860 Census listed forty-one free blacks in Bibb County and three thousand five hundred in Georgia. One of them was Solomon Humphries, known as Free Sol. Born a slave in Jones County he was able to buy his freedom because of his intelligence and determination. He owned the largest store in Bibb County and employed white clerks. He and his wife, Patsy, entertained the leaders of Macon at their home on Broadway. Another free black was Edward Woodliff, a barber. His wife was a slave whose freedom he bought. He owned twelve houses in Macon.

From the 1830s, Northern attacks on slavery increased in number and strength. A young Macon woman, Miss Clare de Graffenreid, wrote articles condemning slavery. But slavery was not an issue in Macon. Almost all whites supported slavery and its expansion into new western territories. What divided people in Macon was the question of whether to remain loyal to the Union or leave it to preserve states' rights.

Simri Rose's newspaper, *The Georgia Journal and Messenger*, supported the Unionist Party. Joseph Clisby's *Macon Daily Telegraph* supported the Democrats. But the election of 1860 marked a change. Although Stephen A. Douglas, the

❖

Left: Joseph Clisby was editor of The Macon Telegraph. He initially opposed secession but was loyal to his state and supported the Confederacy. He promoted calm, order and good sense during the War Between the States and Reconstruction. He was a supporter of public education and president of the Board of Education.

Below: The Lanier House was for decades Macon's premier hotel. Opened by Sidney Lanier's grandparents, its busiest days came during the War Between the States. Jefferson Davis rallied the people of Macon in a speech from its balcony and some months later was brought back as a prisoner of war to face Union General Wilson there. Shortly after the hotel closed in the 1970s the building was demolished.

THE HOTEL LANIER, MACON, GEORGIA.

THE DUVAL, JACKSONVILLE, FLORIDA.
Ethridge, Foor & Company, Props.

❖

Right: In 1866, Rose Hill was the site of Macon's first annual Confederate Memorial Day services. Sidney Lanier was speaker at the exercises which have continued each April for more than one hundred forty years.

Below: Rose Hill Cemetery was created by the city in 1840. Designed by Simri Rose as a garden cemetery, its hills, valleys and terraces constitute the last resting place of thousands of Maconites. Several Confederate generals and more than six hundred Confederate soldiers are buried within its sixty-eight acres.

candidate of the regular Democratic Party, visited Macon just before the election and spoke to a large crowd, Clisby gave his paper's support to the secession Democrat, John C. Breckinridge. In Bibb County three-fifths of the voters chose candidates loyal to the Union, two-fifths chose Breckinridge. No vote went to the candidate who opposed the expansion of slavery and who won the election, Abraham Lincoln.

Lincoln's election immediately ended Macon's loyalty to the Union. Less than a month later, when word reached Macon that South Carolina had seceded, one hundred guns fired a salute, church bells rang, and fifteen hundred people marched in a torch-light parade. Washington Poe led a town meeting which called for citizens to "organize and arm themselves", and for a state convention to decide what Georgia should do.

Above: Rose Hill Cemetery's history, natural beauty, and fine examples of funerary art continue to make it a popular destination for Macon citizens as well as visitors from distant places.

Below: In 1865 Rose Hill still had two lakes which became bathing facilities for occupying Union troops. Macon ladies visiting the graves of their loved ones were scandalized by the sight of nearly naked men frolicking in the water. The lakes were subsequently drained.

That convention was held in Milledgeville in January. Washington Poe, John B. Lamar, and Eugenius A. Nisbet were Macon's representatives. Judge Nisbet was one of Macon's most loyal Unionists whose mind had been changed by Lincoln's election. The convention chose him to write an ordinance of secession, a document to declare Georgia independent of the United States. He was also made a delegate to the Montgomery, Alabama, convention which created a new, Southern government, The Confederate States of America.

Afraid that Lincoln would not allow the Southern states to leave the Union in peace, Macon leaders began to organize military units. Macon's two oldest corps, the Macon Volunteers and the Floyd Rifles, were joined by many new corps. Any man or group who had some experience, money, and volunteers could organize a unit. After Fort Sumter at Charleston fell to Confederate forces in April, 1861, Macon's military corps set out for Virginia or the Georgia coast.

During the war no complete records were kept of the number of Macon men who served. That number was estimated to be about two thousand. Between three hundred fifty and five hundred Macon men died as a result of the war. One killed in action was John Basil Lamar. He was owner of several farms, but lived in Macon in the house built by Ambrose Baber. As a young man he was a private in the

Above: In 1871 Mercer College relocated from Penfield, Georgia. In its early days the entire college was housed in what is now the administration building for Mercer University.

Below: Mercer was situated facing Tattnal Square Park, Macon's original northwest commons and the end of the streetcar line.

Right: The date of construction of the Macon Volunteers Armory is inscribed on its parapet. The military troop which built it participated in all wars through World War II. Above its Gothic arch main door are terra cotta masks of Robert E. Lee and Thomas J. (Stonewall) Jackson.

Below: Since his death in 1863 Elam Alexander's bequest has subsidized public education in Macon. Alexander I, the first of four schools to bear his name, was located on First Street.

Florida Seminole War of 1835. He was an early believer in secession and a delegate to Georgia's secession convention. In the war he served on the staff of his brother-in-law, General Howell Cobb. He was killed defending a pass at Crampton's Gap, Virginia.

General Edward Dorr Tracy, Jr. was another Macon native who died in battle. The son of Macon's early leader moved to Alabama shortly before the war. He fought at the First Battle of Manassas and at Shiloh. In May 1863, he was killed at Port Gibson, Mississippi.

A naval officer from Georgia's coast, Captain John McIntosh Kell, married a Macon girl, Blanche Munroe. Captain Kell was an officer with Commodore Perry on his 1854 trip to Japan. When the war began he resigned from the United States Navy and served as First Mate on the Confederate warship, The *Alabama*. His ship sank sixty Union ships before it was sunk near the end of the war. Captain Kell survived the war and returned to his wife in Macon.

Another Confederate volunteer from Macon was Sidney Lanier. At age nineteen he went to Virginia to serve in the army of Robert E. Lee. He was captured by Union forces and imprisoned at a camp in Maryland. The unhealthy conditions at the camp caused a serious illness from which Lanier never recovered. Despite his illness, after the war Lanier wrote poetry and music which earned him a national reputation.

While little actual fighting came to Macon during the War Between the States the town was very much a center of war activity. South Georgia farmers grew much of the food for the

In 1874, Macon's Jewish community constructed this handsome synagogue on First Street. Since before the War Between the States Jewish people have contributed to Macon's business and civic activities.

Confederate armies. Most of the food supplies passed through the rail center of Macon. Captured Union prisoners passed through on the way to prison camps in South Georgia. On the fair grounds south of town, Macon had its own prison camp for union officers. It was named Camp Oglethorpe and almost one thousand prisoners were held there. Many of them died of disease and at least three were killed while trying to escape.

The Confederate Government took over Findlay's Foundry and made it an armory where five hundred workers made cannons, shot and shells. Other Macon factories switched from peacetime goods to make products for the armies. They produced swords, buttons, wire, soap and matches. In 1862 a Confederate arsenal was moved from Savannah to Macon and large quantities of arms and ammunition were stored there. One of Macon's most successful businessmen, William Butler Johnston, was made a regional treasurer of the Confederate Government. He was in charge of one and a half million dollars in gold kept at Macon which was the largest amount kept outside the Confederate capital at Richmond.

The women of Macon helped in the effort to win the war. Mrs. Washington Poe headed the Ladies' Soldiers' Relief Society, which made bandages and clothes for sick and wounded soldiers. Large numbers of wounded soldiers began to arrive in Macon after the 1862 Battle of Sharpsburg in Maryland. A group of women bought the old Macon Hotel and made it into the Wayside Home, a hotel, hospital, and food center for sick and disabled soldiers. Martha Cook Winship, daughter of the old Fort Hawkins commander, used her own home as a Confederate hospital. She wrote hundreds of letters to relatives of her patients and marked the graves of those who died.

After 1862 the war brought ever more changes to the lives of Macon people. By early 1863 a Confederate dollar was worth one-fiftieth of its 1861 value. The Union Navy's success in stopping ships from entering or leaving Southern ports made many goods impossible to get in the South. Joseph Clisby's newspaper advised Macon people to make moccasins to wear instead of shoes. Blind Tom, a famous black pianist, played in Macon and gave the mayor several hundred pounds of food for use by soldiers' families.

As other parts of the South came under the control of Union troops Macon seemed to be a place of safety. Young girls from all over the South were sent to Macon girls' schools. Women with young children arrived to stay with relatives and friends. Confederate wounded filled all Macon's hospitals. Surgeon-General James Mercer Green used his own home as a hospital and persuaded others to do the same. Hotels, churches, and public buildings were used to house the wounded. By late 1864 more than six thousand wounded were in Macon. Newspapers described the food situation as desperate. Competing for food with citizens, slaves, soldiers, visitors and prisoners was a large group of people who camped near the railroad. The campers were described as "thieves, drunks, deserters, and loose women".

Jefferson Davis, president of the Confederacy, came to Macon late in 1863. He spoke to a large crowd from the balcony of the Lanier House hotel. His positive talk gave his listeners new hope they needed badly. A few months later Macon faced its first attack by the enemy.

During the summer of 1864 Atlanta was threatened by Union General Sherman. Atlanta citizens, hospitals, and newspapers moved to Macon. To keep Macon safe, General Lee sent Georgia's General Howell Cobb to set up headquarters in the town.

Late in July Sherman's Lieutenant-General Stoneman made a raid on Macon. Georgia's governor, Joseph E. Brown, was in Macon when word came of Stoneman's approach with a force of twenty-five hundred men. The governor ordered every citizen with a gun to gather in Macon's defense. Those who gathered were sick soldiers, young boys and old men.

Stoneman fired cannonballs into Macon from the Dunlap farm, site of the Indian Mounds, on the east bank of the river. One struck the home of Judge Asa Holt damaging a column and crashing into the house.

Macon was lucky that an 800-man Tennessee company and a 1,000-man state militia company were passing through town at the time of Stoneman's raid. With the local volunteers they made a stand at Walnut Creek. Stoneman was fooled into thinking Macon was protected by a much larger force, and so retreated. Confederate losses were light, but one was a sixteen year old boy, Michael Barfield. Wounded in the fighting, he was carried to a nearby cabin where he died before his parents could reach him. Stoneman did what damage he could in the area east of Macon, but after three days he was captured. Macon remained safe.

In November, Macon learned that Sherman had burned Atlanta and was marching southeast. His army was spread out on a path sixty miles wide and was taking or destroying everything in its path that could be useful to the Confederacy. Sherman headed for the state capital at Milledgeville, sending General Kirkpatrick to take Macon. Again, the main battle was at Walnut Creek near the Dunlap farm and, again, the union forces retreated. Confederate losses were heavier there and at nearby Griswoldville. But, again, Macon remained safe.

State officials escaped as Sherman took Milledgeville. The legislature met in Macon in February, 1865. City Hall, which had been built as a bank and was later used as a cotton warehouse, became the temporary state capitol. Sherman hoped by his march of destruction to destroy Georgia's will to fight. In Macon a group

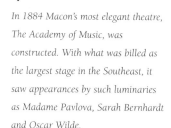

In 1884 Macon's most elegant theatre, The Academy of Music, was constructed. With what was billed as the largest stage in the Southeast, it saw appearances by such luminaries as Madame Pavlova, Sarah Bernhardt and Oscar Wilde.

Among Macon's industries which were part of the town's "New South" identity was the Acme Brewing Company, manufacturers of Macon beer in the pre-prohibition era.

led by former mayor James H. R. Washington wanted Georgia to make peace. General Cobb spoke to the people and convinced them to continue to fight.

By early April, realizing that the South had no resources to continue the war, Confederate General Lee surrendered to Union General Grant. A few days later Generals Johnston and Sherman signed an agreement to end the fighting. In Macon General Cobb was informed of the agreement, but Union General James H. Wilson in Columbus was not. There he destroyed factories, railroads, buildings, and cotton, and then set out for Macon where he planned to do the same.

For the third time in nine months the people of Macon prepared to be attacked. Some tried to escape. A train was loaded with people who carried what belongings they could. Some sat on the roofs of the cars. The train, moving very slowly, almost reached Barnesville when broken tracks forced it to return to Macon.

Cobb sent word of the peace agreement to Wilson who refused to accept the news from a Confederate. Cobb therefore surrendered the town. He persuaded Wilson to have his 13,500 men camp at Tatnall Square rather than march into Macon. A smaller force was sent into town and, as they approached City Hall, they shot a Confederate guard on the porch making him the only fatality in battle inside the town during the war.

To prevent the kind of burning that had happened in other cities General Cobb ordered that all the whiskey in Macon be poured into the streets. Even so, two blocks of Mulberry Street were burned by Union soldiers. General Wilson moved into the mansion built by Jerry Cowles on the hill overlooking the town. He placed Howell Cobb under arrest at his own house. Governor Brown met with General Wilson and surrendered to him the troops of the Georgia Militia. General Wilson became the only person in Macon with the power to make or enforce law.

The war was over. Macon was defeated, but not destroyed.

CHAPTER IV

TOWN OF THE NEW SOUTH

At the end of the War Between the States Macon was not in ruins. Most of its citizens lived through the war, most of its buildings still stood; but, in many ways Macon had reached its lowest point. A well-known writer of the time, Bret Harte, visited Macon and wrote of it in a letter: "But my dominant impression—above everything—is one of sadness…the wasted, ill-kept fields, the scattered negro cabins, the decaying and fallen plantations, the badly dressed people and hopeless negro…all are pathetic". It took many years for the town to recover to the point of health and wealth it knew in 1860.

Many of Macon's young men died in the war. Others lost eyes, arms, legs, or their mental health. The war's end meant that people who owned slaves lost all the value invested in them. The slaves became freedmen, but had no jobs, homes, education, or experience in getting them. The only money most people had was worthless Confederate currency. The former leaders of the town had no power or means of getting it. In spite of these and other problems, Macon recovered.

Macon's most noted author in the late Nineteenth and early Twentieth Centuries was Harry Stillwell Edwards. He was a columnist for The Macon Telegraph, *an essayist and a quite successful novelist. He did his writing in Kingfisher Cabin, a retreat on his family plantation, Holly Bluff. The cabin is now an attraction on the grounds of Macon's Museum of Arts and Sciences.*

In 1889, local architect D. B. Woodruff designed the first building built to house Macon's public library. The Macon Heritage Foundation preserved it from demolition. Its two-story reading room with oak ship's beam rafters and clerestory windows is intact and the building has been restored.

Macon's military governor, General Wilson, was given the name Spooney in Virginia because his men were known for taking private property, especially silverware. However, when he took the house owned by Mrs. Bond for his use she asked him to see that her valuables were untouched. Months later, when she was allowed to return she was pleased to find nothing missing.

Stealing did become a serious problem as the war ended. Soldiers, or other hungry people, stole chickens and livestock from people's yards at night. Citizens took turns patrolling their neighborhoods from dusk until sunrise.

General Wilson hung a large American flag in front of his office on Mulberry Street. One morning a young Macon man and three young ladies, all members of the Ross family, walked by. They stepped off the sidewalk into the street rather than walk under the flag, the symbol of the enemy. Soldiers stopped and questioned them and the young man was made to pace under the flag for a half-hour.

In May 1865, a search party sent by General Wilson captured Confederate President, Jefferson Davis, in south Georgia. Hundreds of people gathered at the Lanier House to watch as Davis was brought there to face Wilson. Neither the Macon people nor the Union soldiers made any sound as the captive was led into the hotel where he had once spoken to cheering crowds. Wilson treated Davis with courtesy, but he was sent to prison and made to wear chains for two years.

Howell Cobb also was arrested and put on a train for Washington, D.C. General Wilson telegraphed the Secretary of War that unless Cobb was released, he, Wilson, would resign

from the army. Cobb was quickly returned to Macon. People in Macon wrote that Wilson treated them kindly. Years after the war when he visited in Macon its people treated him kindly and made him welcome.

Under General Wilson's rule Macon slowly began to return to normal. Stephen Collins was allowed to resume his duties as mayor. J. H. R. Washington was appointed Postmaster. Two days after Macon fell newspapers were printed. The same day Macon's leading theatre, Ralston Hal, was reopened. Tickets sold for food rather than money. One month later citizens were allowed for the first time to leave town without a pass.

While some things returned to normal others were changed forever. The slaves were free. Shortly after the war the first schools were opened for freedmen. Classes were held in houses, churches, even barns. Most of the teachers were Northerners or blacks who were free before the war.

In 1866 Macon was governed by a Provost Marshall who enforced his orders with Federal troops. Most of his time was spent dealing with the complaints and requests of freedmen who crowded his office each day.

The Federal troops were removed from Macon in the summer of 1868. Two years later Georgia was officially brought back into the union. As democracy slowly returned the government was controlled by carpetbaggers, Northerners who came South after the war, and by scalawags, Southerners who worked with the carpetbaggers. Blacks held some offices. Pulaski Holt, a merchant, Edward Woodliff, a barber, and Henderson Dumas became the first black members of Macon's City Council. A convention called to write a new constitution for Georgia was controlled by 108 scalawags, 9 carpetbaggers, and 37 blacks.

Above: Macon's streetcars initially were pulled by mules, then by steam locomotives, until electric power was developed. The town's growth followed the street car lines.

Below: Crump's Park was a popular privately-owned recreation area at the far end of the Vineville street car line. It featured ponds, a casino, a theatre, and a dance pavilion.

Chapter IV ◆ 35

Above: In 1879, John W. Burke published his History of Macon and Central Georgia *which became a foundation for all future historians of the town. Burke also wrote a biography of his former employer, Elam Alexander, and operated a printing business which offered books and stationery.*

Below: The closing of the J. W. Burke Printing Company in 1891 was more of a loss to Macon's literary scene than to its economy.

In 1868 war hero Ulysses S. Grant was elected president. He appointed Henry M. Turner, a black preacher, postmaster of Macon. White Macon leaders asked Grant to cancel the appointment. Grant agreed, but then allowed Turner to take office. After only two weeks Turner was removed for reasons of "gross immorality," although records did not explain what Turner was accused of doing.

In the election of 1872, Jeff Long, a black leader of Georgia Republicans, spoke to a crowd at the city hall. Democrats gathered, arguments started, and a riot followed. Four people were killed and many injured.

The war, military rule, and the reign of the carpetbaggers resulted in hard feelings that lasted a long time in Georgia. In 1884 Grover Cleveland was elected the first Democrat to be president since before the war. The celebration that followed his election was called "the largest ever seen in Macon", with more than ten thousand people joyfully filling the streets. When blacks and Republicans lost power in the state government Georgia became a one party state giving solid support to Democrats for more than a century.

After the war, Macon people were anxious to help the town rebuild and recover. In Atlanta a newspaper editor named Henry W. Grady called for a "New South". He urged farmers to grow crops other than cotton and for businessmen to build factories. Just as Macon had outstanding leaders in its beginning, it had fine leaders at the time of its new beginning. Many of the new leaders agreed with Mr. Grady. Among the new leaders who moved to Macon seeking opportunities were Howell Cobb, Nat E. Harris, A. O. Bacon, and James H. Blount.

Before the War Between the States, Howell Cobb served as Secretary of the Treasury, Speaker of the House of Representatives, and Governor of Georgia. His wife was the sister of

John B. Lamar and she inherited his house in Macon. The Cobbs lived in that house while he was in charge of Macon's war defense. Cobb was a calming force in Macon in the stormy days after the war, but his efforts were cut short by his sudden death in 1868.

Nat E. Harris came to Georgia from Tennessee when the war ended. He practiced law in Macon and was elected to the state legislature in 1882. Believing that the New South needed people trained in science and mechanics he pledged to work for a school of technology for Georgia. In 1885 he succeeded in getting a bill passed to create the Georgia Institute of Technology. In 1915 Harris was elected Governor of Georgia. After serving one term he returned to Macon and his law practice. He was always called the Father of Georgia Tech.

Augustus O. Bacon was a recent graduate of the University of Georgia in 1866 when he came to Macon to practice law. He was first elected to the state legislature in 1871 and, in

❖

Above: In gratitude for his role in leading Macon to recovery from war and Reconstruction, Mayor Price was honored by having Daisy Park and Price Library named for him. The handsome neo-classic building remains although the library closed in the 1970s.

Bottom, left: James H. Blount was among the first Confederate veterans elected to Congress during Reconstruction. After a long career in the House of Representatives he served on government missions to Hawaii, Cuba and the Philippines.

Bottom, left: Mayor Sylvester B. Price was nicknamed "Daisy" because, like the flower, he was a perennial.

Chapter IV ✦ 37

1881, began the first of his five terms as speaker of the Georgia House. In 1896 he was appointed to the United States Senate where he served until his death eighteen years later. At that time he was President Pro Tem of the Senate. In Macon he helped establish a street car line and he donated land for the Masonic Home for orphans and for the Alexander III School. In his will he left his estate, Baconsfield, to Macon for use as a park.

James H. Blount moved from Jones County to Macon in 1865. He was elected to Congress in 1872 and served there for twenty years. As a Congressman, Blount helped to get free mail delivery in Macon and a United States District Court. In 1893 Blount was a special representative to Hawaii where he criticized the United States' role in the overthrow of the queen. After the Spanish-American War, Blount was made Judge Advocate of Cuba and later of the Philippines.

A native of Macon who became one of its most popular mayors was Sylvester B. Price. People in Macon called him Daisy. He was elected mayor in 1882 but resigned to become postmaster in 1883. By the next year he was mayor again and he remained in the office until 1899. His long term of office brought many improvements to Macon. After he had been re-elected several times, *The Macon Telegraph* wrote, "The rose has but a summer's reign, but the Daisy never dies."

Another Macon man who headed many projects to improve the town was Henry Horne. He did as much as any man to bring industry to Macon. He was elected to City Council in 1887, to the mayor's chair in 1893.

Above: Known as the "Father of Georgia Tech", Governor Nat E. Harris early recognized the value of technical and industrial education in the "New South".

Below: The Log Cabin Club was a rural retreat for Macon business and professional men. Located near the present junction of Log Cabin Drive and Napier Avenue, it was a forerunner of the Idle Hour Country Club.

Above: Despite efforts to diversify crops and develop industry in the New South, cotton remained a staple at the turn of the Twentieth Century as indicated by the stack of cotton bales on Poplar Street.

Below: In 1910 Macon acquired its first automotive fire engine. The pride in it shown by the firemen who posed with it would soon be tempered by a fatal accident.

When Macon's best theatre, Ralston Hall, burned, Horne built a new one, The Academy of Music. He served as manager of the new theatre which later became the Grand Opera House. He was a partner in Macon's largest streetcar company and a director of *The Macon Telegraph*.

Above: U. S. District Judge Emory Speer was once dean of Mercer's law school and had a distinguished career on the Federal bench, but was remembered most for his obstinate refusal, in 1903, to vacate his office so that the old courthouse could be demolished and a new one erected.

Below: Macon's major event of 1912 was a reunion of Confederate veterans which attracted hundreds of the former soldiers and thousands to watch the spectacle.

Opposite, top: The dawn of the Twentieth Century in Macon saw a renewed prosperity evidenced by a boom in building. Saint Joseph's Catholic Church was completed in 1903 adjacent to the First Baptist Church at the top of Poplar Street.

Opposite, bottom: New houses along College Street fitted in well with their antebellum neighbors. The aspect of this block is essentially the same as a century ago except for the addition of the Massee Apartments.

He worked to bring to Macon paved streets, sewers, a public hospital, and city parks. His greatest boost to Macon came in 1888 when he spent a year in New York City searching for new industry. He was said to have paid $2,000 for an article in *The New York World* which caused twenty new businesses to locate in Macon.

Another citizen who brought national attention to Macon was Harry Stillwell Edwards. He served as postmaster in Macon but his real contribution was his writing. He wrote for *The Macon Telegraph* and sold articles to national magazines. In 1896 he won a ten thousand dollar prize from a Chicago newspaper for his novel of the New South, *Sons and Fathers*. He used the prize money to buy bicycles for young people in Macon. His most popular work was *Aeneas Africanus*, a short novel about a former slave looking for his master's family after the War Between the States.

Many other citizens of Macon helped in the town's recovery from war. Businessmen who helped create jobs also gave their time and money to good causes. Such men were referred to in Macon as "merchant princes". Among the best known were Isaac Hardeman, Benjamin L. Willingham, T. D. Tinsley, S. R. Jaques, S. T. Coleman, W. A. Huff, Gus Nussbaum, S. S. Dunlap, S. Waxelbaum, and T. C. Burke.

Some citizens found conditions in Macon too discouraging after the war. Sidney Lanier was unable to support his family practicing law. In 1874 he gave a recital at Ralston Hall to raise enough money to take his family to Baltimore. Others joined him in moving north where business was booming in new industries such as steel and oil.

Macon did not boom with business, but slowly the town made progress in its recovery.

Poplar Street, Showing Catholic and Baptist Churches, Macon, Ga.

Residence View on College Street, Macon, Ga.

Another blending of early twentieth century residences with antebellum ones can be seen from New Street looking up Mulberry. This view, too, is little altered.

At the war's end William B. Johnston was elected president of the Central Railroad and the rebuilding of the wrecked line to Savannah was begun. A new bridge across the Ocmulgee replaced one burned during the war. Two new businesses opened, the Gus Bernd Company, a leather factory, and the Dannenberg Company, a department store.

The year 1871 brought Macon three important signs of progress. Large buildings were built at Central City Park to house the Georgia State Fair. Macon's first system of trolleys, or streetcars, began to run between the railroad depot and Tattnall Square. With Macon offering one hundred twenty-five thousand dollars and nine acres of land, Mercer College, formerly at the town of Penfield, accepted the invitation to relocate to the western end of the town's new streetcar line.

In 1872 the state legislature created the Bibb County Board of Education and so gave Macon its first completely public schools. Joseph Clisby was the Board's first president. The public school system included four schools for whites, two for blacks.

During 1876, the year of the nation's hundredth birthday, money was raised in Macon to start a public library and historical society. The same year the Ocmulgee reached its highest level on record, with Central City Park and much of East Macon under water. Railroad and water traffic stopped until the water level went down. The railroads were not hurt by the flood, for by 1880 Macon was the center of more rail lines than any Georgia city. In 1881 forty-nine trains stopped daily in Macon.

The last years of the 1800s saw many improvements in the town. In 1879 electricity became available. In 1880 the town government took charge of the water system. In 1882 telephone service was begun. In 1886 a paid fire department replaced the volunteer organization. In 1887 street signs were put up and houses numbered. In 1894 sewers were laid. In 1895 the Macon Hospital opened as Macon's first public hospital. In 1897, major streets were paved. The same year, Macon got a second bridge to cross the Ocmulgee at Spring Street. In 1897 shipping was begun again on the river with a steamboat called the *City of Macon* making trips to the coast.

Some unusual events happened in Macon in the closing years of the Nineteenth Century. In 1886 record cold froze the Ocmulgee and people were able to walk across it. The same year an earthquake shook windows and chimneys and stopped the clock at the railroad station. In 1887 more than fifty thousand people crowded into Macon for a reunion of Confederate veterans. Jefferson Davis attended and a large ball was given in his honor. In 1896 a Philadelphia man, George Gassler, made possible another industry in Macon when he found, nearby, a white clay called kaolin used in the production of porcelain and slick paper.

Macon's progress in the late 1800s was limited by setbacks. Profits declined in the cotton mills in the late 1880s. In 1891 a depression closed several local banks and businesses, among them the J. W. Burke Printing Company and *The Macon News*. In 1893 the Bibb Mills closed for ten days putting six hundred people out of work. The mills were reopened on half time. In both 1894 and 1895 county tax collections decreased. Conditions began to improve in 1897 and, within two years, two new cotton mills opened, The Willingham and The Ocmulgee.

The 1880 population count showed that twelve thousand five hundred people lived in Macon. The count made the town seem smaller than it was because it did not include people

Above: The Grand Opera House was created in 1906 to enlarge the Academy of Music. The Grand became a movie theatre in the 1930s and closed in the 1960s. Macon theatre lovers united in 1969 to restore the old theatre to its former glory and since then it has been a well-used and much-loved community resource.

Left: In 1916 a new railroad terminal was opened at the foot of Cherry Street. For over fifty years, Terminal Station was a beehive of activity. It is now owned by the City of Macon and may one day serve again as a passenger depot.

◆

Above: A new chapter in Macon's history was opened with the construction of the town's first airfield at Central City Park.

Below: Macon people have always loved parades. Patriotism in World War I stimulated a large turnout for a parade of troops in 1918.

who lived in East Macon, Vineville, or western Bibb County. In 1897 efforts were made to add the surrounding areas to Macon before the census of 1900. A county vote on the issue caused a lively battle. The vote failed and the areas were not added. Even so, Macon's population in 1900 had risen to more than twenty-three thousand.

The slow return of local control of local government and of financial good health helped ease the bitterness Macon had known in the years that followed the War Between the States. But it was another war which restored national pride in Macon. The war was fought with Spain in 1898.

When the Unites States ship, The Maine, exploded in the harbor at Havana, Cuba, newspapers across the country blamed Spain and demanded action. The Macon Telegraph advised a calm investigation of the explosion, but when the United States went to war Macon gave its total support. Macon volunteer units, the old Macon Volunteers and Floyd Rifles among them, left to train for war. Two black units were included. Macon's women started a new Soldiers' Relief Association. In the Philippines, Macon's Lieutenant Emory Winship, though hit by five bullets, manned a machine gun to save one hundred twenty-five men. His hometown presented him with a jeweled sword.

After a quick American victory, eight army companies were sent to camps at Macon to adjust before being discharged. In December, 1898, President William McKinley visited Macon to inspect the camps. He spoke to a large, friendly crowd, telling them it was "time to heal old wounds." The people of Macon seemed to agree.

As the old century ended, Macon was not looking backward, but ahead to a new century in which growth would be greater than anything in its past.

❖

Above: The creation of Camp Wheeler had the greatest impact on Macon during World War I. It was dismantled at war's end, rebuilt during World War II.

Below: Mrs. C. C. Harrold's automobile is a symbol of her status as a 1920s "modern woman." She obviously balanced her role as mother with her achievements in politics and public health.

Chapter IV ♦ 45

❖

Right: A view of Macon's main shopping venue, Cherry Street, shows its vibrancy in an aerial view, c. 1950.

Below: An artist's view of the Macon skyline in 1923.

CHAPTER V

TWENTIETH CENTURY CITY

A New York magazine in 1906 described Macon as one of the "most Southern of all old Southern towns". The twentieth century began quietly in Macon. Its people did not expect the events, sometimes stormy ones, which changed the old Southern town into a modern American city. Later, people remembered the early 1900s as a time of peace and comfort, of slow growth and gradual change.

Macon's major dispute of 1903 showed how little it took to upset people. Congress approved the building of a new post office on the site of the old Federal Courthouse. Judge Emory Speer refused to move out of his office to allow the old courthouse to be torn down. After several months of delay, the government began to consider an idea of tearing down all the building except the Judge's office. After two years, President Theodore Roosevelt issued an order that the contract be carried out, and the entire building was torn down. Judge Speer got the last word by adjourning court until, he said, he had a new courtroom.

Other events at the turn of the century reflected gentle changes. In 1900 Macon's last public well was sealed. The same year a new library opened named for Mayor Daisy Price who died the year before.

❖

A gift of land and money from Mrs. Ellen Washington Bellamy in memory of her brother Hugh Vernon Washington was responsible for the construction of the Washington Memorial Library, completed in 1923.

Chapter V ✦ 47

❖

Above In 1925 the new City Auditorium was dedicated as a memorial to soldiers from Macon who had served in World War I. It boasted an auditorium which could seat sixty-five hundred people. Above the stage was a mural painted by Don Carlos DuBois and Wilbur Kurtz depicting Macon's history, 1540 to 1920. Above it all was a copper dome said to have been the largest in the world.

Below: In 1928 the growth of Wesleyan College led to development of a new campus, Greater Wesleyan, at Rivoli on Macon's outskirts. The new site afforded more than 130 acres for expansion and development, a movement continuing in the twenty-first century.

A small event at the time, but one what would change Macon greatly in later years, was the introduction of the automobile in 1901. Four steam-powered locomobiles were brought to Macon for sale. They held two people, had engines of five horsepower, and traveled at speeds up to thirty miles per hour.

In 1910 Macon bought its first automobile fire engine. Within a month three firemen were killed when a tire blew and the engine crashed. Despite the accident, by 1913 all horse-drawn engines had been replaced by self-powered ones.

Between 1900 and World War I the areas of Vineville, Huguenin Heights, East Macon, and South Macon were annexed into the city. Macon's city government provided new and better services to the townspeople. It created a Board of Health, added a public auditorium to City Hall, and opened four supervised playgrounds. All city parks were named and marked with signs. The Macon Hospital added a new wing and a school for nurses. Cherry Street was the first to be lighted with electricity and was called "The Great White Way."

In 1916, after ruining cotton farms in other parts of the south, the boll weevil arrived in Georgia. New South leaders had tried for years to get Georgia farmers to stop depending on cotton and turn to other crops. The devastation caused by the boll weevil made that happen.

Macon women were heard from in 1914. A large crowd of them met at the new City Hall Auditorium to hear Mrs. W. S. Stener of Washington, D.C., demand the right to vote for women. That year two Macon women—Mrs. Robert Smith and her daughter, Miss Ruth Smith—were in France when it was invaded by Germany. They stayed to nurse the wounded in the war.

During events leading to the First World War Macon showed its military spirit. After a 1916 clash between United States' troops and Mexicans, Georgia's governor from Macon, Nat Harris, alerted the state's National Guard. The governor's son, General Walter A. Harris, headed the guard. He summoned it to train in Macon at Camp Harris on the Forsyth Road. Three companies of these Macon-trained troops went to duty in Texas. They returned to Camp Harris in January, 1917. That same month General Leonard Wood came to Georgia looking for a site for an army training camp. He chose Holly Bluff,

a plantation east of Macon owned by author Harry Stillwell Edwards.

President Woodrow Wilson asked Congress to declare war on April 6, 1917. By June the first of sixty thousand troops began arriving at the new Camp Wheeler, named for General Joseph A. Wheeler who was an officer in both the Confederate and the United States Army. One battalion of troops trained at Camp Wheeler was made up of Macon and other Georgia companies. It was named the 151st Machine Gun Battalion and it suffered heavy losses fighting in France.

Many of the camp's trainees did not make it to war. A large number died of measles, pneumonia, or Spanish influenza. As diseases spread all of the people at the camp were required to wear masks. Early in 1918 conditions grew worse when a severe flood wrecked the camp. A hard freeze following the flood made cleaning up the wreckage impossible for a time.

The town of Macon was filled with war spirit. Central City Park became a camp for military police. Citizens planted war gardens to save food for the fighting men. Mrs. R. L. Berner, chairman of the Bibb County Food Conservation Commission, called on Macon people to have meatless days and sugarless days. To save fuel, lightless nights were held. Macon's eight cotton mills closed for five days, and electric street cars were pulled by horses.

Macon's Red Cross, its Young Women's Christian Association, and all its churches worked to support the war effort. Local high schools and Mercer University began offering military classes. Comedian Charlie Chaplin visited Macon selling Liberty Bonds to help pay for the war. In one week Macon people bought more than a million dollars worth of bonds. A parade to show Macon's war spirit was fifteen miles long. It took three hours to pass the platform from which Governor Harris watched.

On the day the war ended, according to *The Macon Telegraph*, "The town went mad." Before dawn three huge bonfires lit the downtown streets. Every type of noise-maker, from a fiddle to a cannon, was used to celebrate the victory. As seven brass bands played, people crowded the streets all day.

The month after the war ended Camp Wheeler was closed. Within weeks the buildings were taken apart and removed and the land was cleared.

The end of 1920s prosperity enjoyed by Macon was foreshadowed by the collapse of the Fourth National Bank in 1928. False rumors led to a run on the bank causing many depositors to lose their money.

After the World War, Macon joined the rest of the country in a period of rapid change. In the Roaring Twenties people began to live in very different ways. In Georgia, the boll weevil and low farm prices caused many farmers to move into towns. Farm life meant work that was never finished, but town life allowed time for entertainment. In the '20s, new inventions cut time and distance. Women gained new freedom. The pace of life in the old Southern town of Macon grew faster.

New public buildings proved that Macon was doing well. In 1923 the Washington Memorial Library was opened and, in 1924, the new courthouse was completed. The next year the new Municipal Auditorium could seat 6,500 people, and a new athletic stadium could seat 12,000.

By 1920 Macon's first truck line was in business. Trucks and a rapidly growing number of cars created demands for better roads. By 1925 Macon had 31 miles of paved streets and Bibb County had 72 miles of paved roads. Soon after the first traffic lights were installed automobiles had changed the way people lived in Macon. New suburbs grew quickly. People could drive to downtown jobs from new houses

Above: As the country sank into the Great Depression people in Macon, as elsewhere, sought escape from unpleasant realities at the movies. A crowd gathered under the marquee at the Capitol Theatre emblazoned with the hopeful line "Happy Days Are Here Again."

Below: Federal work programs funded landscaping, foot paths, and an elaborate water course at Washington Park on Magnolia Street. Springs in this hillside provided water for Macon's original waterworks. Strictly supervised Wesleyan students from the college's old campus across College Street were allowed to talk to boys in the park on Sunday afternoons (under the watchful eyes of chaperones). For that reason the Wesleyannes called the park "Paradise."

in Shirley Hills, Cherokee Heights, Stanislaus, and Ingleside.

An air show was held in 1919 at Central City Park. A plane took off carrying mail to Montgomery, Alabama, beginning air mail service for Macon. By 1926 the old parade ground at Camp Wheeler had become a regular stop on the air mail route. Macon's air travel had a brief setback in 1927 when a plane crashed on busy Cherry Street. Killed were the pilot, a passenger, and a man on the sidewalk.

Radio came to Macon in 1922 when Mercer University started the first station. Its call letters, WMAZ, stood for "Watch Mercer Attain Zenith," meaning reach the highest point. Radio became an important source of information and a popular form of entertainment for Macon.

Organized sports became another favorite form of entertainment in 1920s Macon. Mercer's football team filled the city's new stadium when they played there. Macon's baseball team, the Peaches, played in a new sixty thousand dollar ball park. A local boxer, W. L. Stribling, brought attention to Macon. Known as Young Stribling, he won two hundred ninety fights before losing a world championship match in 1931.

Macon's four motion picture theatres lost little business when the price of tickets doubled from a nickel to a dime. Macon people enjoyed live performances of a newly organized symphony orchestra made up of local musicians. Several amateur theatre groups staged plays. In the late '20s a grand opera company performed annually in Macon.

The 1920s provided little social or political equality for blacks in Macon, but black shoppers did have the choice of shopping at the twenty-two stores owned by blacks. L. H. Douglass operated two theatres for blacks, one for movies, one for live performances. Macon blacks owned a weekly newspaper, an insurance company, and two banks.

Good things came to Macon from the 1920s civic club movement. Members joining the Kiwanis, Rotary, and Lions Clubs worked to improve the community. The Junior Chamber of Commerce raised funds to furnish the new library and took over the operation of WMAZ.

Women organized similar clubs for themselves. In 1921 Macon women started The Pilot Club for business and professional women. Its great success made it the basis for a network

❖

Above: During World War II, Macon again experienced a sizeable influx of soldiers. Macon people again worked to make them feel welcome and appreciated. One U.S.O. location was at St. Joseph's Church. Here, Miss Susan Myrick, a fascinating story teller, is surrounded by young soldiers. Miss Myrick was a reporter for The Macon Telegraph *and served as technical consultant for the making of the movie* Gone With the Wind.

Below: Mayor Charles Bowden was a dynamo working for Macon from 1938 to 1948. He eliminated the city's debt and had the vision to purchase land at nearby Wellston which was passed on to the Federal Government for creation of an air depot which would become Robins Air Force Base.

Chapter V ♦ 51

Life in Macon's warm climate was changed considerably by the arrival of air conditioning after World War II. Starting with theatres and businesses it was adopted by eager homeowners. After the Rialto Theatre on Cotton Avenue closed its owner left its handsome façade while taking the interior space for use as a parking lot.

of Pilot Clubs across the country. Its success also inspired the creation of a similar Macon organization, The Business and Professional Women's Club.

Some women celebrated their new freedom by cutting their hair or shortening their skirts, but more serious women got involved in politics. In 1919 the Nineteenth Amendment to the Constitution gave women the right to vote. Women in Macon quickly put their new right to use. In 1921 Mrs. Charles C. Harrold became the first woman member of Macon's City Council. She served for many years and made many contributions, especially in the field of public health. She arranged for physical examinations for school children and inspections of meat and dairy products sold in Macon.

Viola Ross Napier, granddaughter of Macon pioneer Simri Rose, was one of the first women to practice law in Macon. In 1922 she became the first woman elected to the Georgia General Assembly. There she worked for badly needed prison reforms in the state. Later, Mrs. Napier served for many years as City Clerk.

The election of women to important offices proved that Macon voters believed women were equal to the job. Macon's long tradition of supporting equal rights for women began with the first women's college. By 1928 so many women wanted to attend Wesleyan that the college decided to expand. A new campus was built at Rivoli, near Macon, and the original College Street building was reserved for students of the fine arts.

In the same year Macon got a preview of the terrible financial problems ahead. The Fourth National Bank, one of Macon's largest, failed after false rumors caused people to withdraw their money. The failure of the bank caused the collapse of seven smaller banks in nearby towns.

The 1929 crash of the stock market began the nation's longest and worst depression. In Macon, as across the country, businesses and industries closed, reduced hours, or laid off workers. Money and jobs were hard to find. Macon's government worked with the federal government to provide jobs. Franklin D. Roosevelt's New Deal programs put Macon people to work repairing City Hall, rebuilding the jail, expanding the Macon Hospital, and building a new airport. These programs gave a total of more than five million man hours of work to Macon's unemployed.

The excavation of the Indian Mounds was another government work project. Experts were brought to Macon to oversee the digging and to record and preserve what was found. The project gave jobs to hundreds while uncovering the history of the people who built the mounds. The federal government acquired the land which had once been the Ocmulgee Old Fields and made it the Ocmulgee National Monument. A museum was built to house what was discovered so that the public could learn the story of the Indians.

Work programs gave relief to many without jobs, but did not end the depression. World War II brought recovery to Macon and the country. Because of the war Macon grew more and faster than ever before. As fighting began in Europe and Asia, Macon's city government bought land near Wellston in Houston County. When the United States entered the war, Macon gave the land to the federal government. In 1941 the government built an air depot there and named it Warner Robins in honor of a World War I Air Corps General. Macon's Mayor Charles L. Bowden and Congressman Carl Vinson deserve credit for bringing this asset to Middle Georgia.

In 1940 City Council created the Macon War Defense Council for the purpose of bringing defense industries to Macon. The same year Macon's National Guard unit was called to active duty. Well before the Japanese attacked Pearl Harbor, Macon was preparing for war.

When war came Macon again geared up to help win victory. The Macon Volunteers, the oldest Macon company, was among the first to join the war effort. In the war years Macon citizens bought more than twenty-two million dollars of war bonds and stamps. They collected two hundred three thousand pounds of scrap metal for defense use. They trained as volunteer air raid wardens, policemen, firefighters, and ambulance drivers. They joined in city-wide

Del Ward became a Macon broadcasting institution. Shown in 1950 behind her customary microphone she worked in radio before pioneering in local television in 1954. Her Southern charm and professional poise have endeared her to generations of Macon listeners and viewers.

Above: In March of 1963 civil rights marchers gathered outside Macon's City Hall. A boycott led to integration of city buses and continuing efforts put an end to segregation in other areas including public education.

Below: Excitement came to Macon with the creation of Capricorn Records by local boy Phil Walden. He made international stars of his artists such as Otis Redding and the Allman Brothers Band.

blackouts for air defense. Women worked in factories, organizations entertained the troops, and ten thousand Macon citizens served in the armed forces.

Macon gave a lot to the war effort and the war effort gave a lot to Macon. Five military projects helped Macon erase the effects of the depression. Camp Wheeler was reopened and rebuilt. A new road named for the camp commander, General Emery, was built to connect the camp to Macon. More than two hundred seventeen thousand men were trained at Camp Wheeler. Building costs alone brought Macon more than ten million dollars.

Five million dollars came to Macon from construction of a government plant to make fuses for explosives. It employed eight thousand people. Cochran Field, a flyers' training school, cost two million dollars. Among those trained there were flyers from Britain's Royal Air Force. A project that cost one million dollars was the expansion of the city's air field for use by the government.

By far the largest government project was the Army Air Corps Depot at Warner Robins. Its construction employed three thousand workers and cost fifteen million dollars. When completed it employed fifteen thousand civilian workers. At the war's end, the government withdrew from the other military projects, but the air depot was expanded. It became a materials center and air base. The town of Warner Robins grew up next to it, but Macon continued to enjoy rich benefits from its military neighbor.

Figures reveal the effects of World War II on Macon. In 1940, Macon industries employed six thousand people. In 1948 the figure had risen to twenty thousand. In 1940, Macon's population was close to 58,000 people, in 1950 more than 70,000. World War II brought to Macon some of the tragedies that result from any war, but it also brought a new era of growth.

In the second half of the twentieth century Macon earned the right to be called a city. The population inside the city limits grew to more than 125,000 people. In ways other than numbers Macon became more like a city and less like a large town. While remaining a farming center, Macon also became a center of business, industry, transportation and culture.

Large industries that came to Macon soon after World War II included Georgia Kraft Company and Inland Container Corporation. Later, efforts to attract industry brought Brown and Williamson Tobacco Company and Y.K.K. Zipper Company to Macon. Y.K.K. was the first of three Japanese manufacturers to locate in Macon. Japanese people who came with those industries helped mix a bit of Oriental flavor into Macon's culture. The Insurance Company of North America and the Government Employees Insurance Company opened headquarters in Macon. A local firm, Charter Medical Corporation, grew to be one of the country's largest hospital management organizations. A company that brought excitement to Macon in the late 1960s and early 1970s was Capricorn Records. The company produced records for top recording artists such as Otis Redding and the Allman Brothers' Band. In the 1960s a civic center was built near the Ocmulgee River. A venue for conventions, sports events and performances of all kinds, the original Macon Coliseum was expanded in the 1990s to become the Centreplex. The old Macon Hospital became the Medical Center of Central Georgia, a huge medical complex. With the expansion of it and the Coliseum Medical Center Macon became a regional destination for medical treatment of all kinds.

In 1982 Macon's first annual Cherry Blossom Festival was held. The city can boast more than three hundred thousand yoshino cherry trees which, around the third week of March, provide a soft pink background for the whole city. The event attracts thousands of visitors from around the nation and, indeed, the world.

In the 1970s Macon joined the burgeoning national historic preservation movement. The Middle Georgia Historical Society and the Intown Macon Neighborhood Association created the Macon Heritage Foundation to preserve Macon's architectural and historical treasures. In 2002 the Historical Society and the Heritage Foundation merged to form the Historic Macon Foundation which continues to preserve and revitalize.

Although Macon's original highway, the Ocmulgee River, was last used for transportation in the 1930s and railroad passenger traffic ended in 1971, Macon remained a transportation center. Macon's airport became a crossroads for regional air traffic. Interstates 16 and 75, two links of the federal interstate highway network, met at Macon and made it a crossroads of highway traffic.

In 1986 Wesleyan College celebrated 150 years as the oldest chartered college for women. In 1968 Macon Junior College was created as the city's unit of the state university system. Mercer University added schools of medicine, engineering, and business in Macon, and expanded to include a branch of the university in Atlanta.

In 1984, as the Grand Opera House observed its centennial, Macon's very successful Little Theatre celebrated its fiftieth anniversary. Arts organizations formed in later years included two concert series, two ballet companies, a local symphony orchestra, a second community theatre group, and a museum of black history. The Museum of Arts and Sciences, created in the 1960s, was expanded in the 1980s to include a planetarium and permanent displays of art and natural science.

As Macon became a city it grew in many senses, but it also faced many problems. Two of the most difficult the city had to face were the achievement of civil rights for its black citizens and the reversal of the decay of its downtown.

Until changes were made in the 1960s blacks and whites in Macon were separate and unequal. The races did not mix in theatres, hotels, restaurants, buses or trains. No black children could attend a white school. Blacks were discouraged from voting and no black held public office.

The movement for equal rights for blacks was several years old before it had an impact in Macon. In 1962 blacks, who were the main customers of the public bus system, refused to ride in buses for over a month. Losses suffered by the bus company caused a change in its policy and, at the end of the boycott, blacks could sit where they wanted on public buses.

On the road to mutual success Phil Walden hands Otis Redding keys to a new convertible. Tragically Redding's career was cut short by a fatal plane crash in 1967

In 1963, forty-four black individuals sued the Board of Education to force the end of separation by race in the public schools. Separation of the races in other public places ended immediately in 1964 when Congress passed a law to make it illegal. Blacks could then eat in any restaurant or stay in any hotel, but schools in Macon were still divided by race. In 1969 a federal judge ordered an immediate end of that situation. In 1970, Macon's high schools were organized as three complexes with no school identified as white or black.

In 1971, Macon had, for the first time, a school board that was elected rather than appointed. Initially two black members were elected to serve on it. Among the courageous leaders who worked to achieve integration in Macon certain names appear repeatedly. They include William P. Randall, Ozzie Belle McKay, Reverend Van Malone, Reverend Julius Hope, Hester Bivins, Thomas Jackson, Emma Lucas, William S. Hutchings, and Dr. D. T. Walton, Jr.

Laws, court orders, and elections did not end racial problems in Macon, but they made it possible for blacks to continue to make progress in the march toward equality.

By the middle years of the 1970s Macon's downtown was dying. Major stores and small shops were moving to outlying shopping centers and a large new shopping mall. What had been, since its earliest days, the active heart of the city was almost deserted. People afraid of crime would not walk the empty sidewalks in front of vacant buildings. As the value of downtown property dropped, the local government lost money from taxes. Many once-fine houses in the area bordering downtown had become neglected, poorly-kept apartments or businesses. Some houses stood empty, some were torn down. Macon was in danger of becoming an expanding city with a rotten center.

City officials saw that the downtown had to be saved. The city government, the federal government, and private citizens worked together to bring life back to the downtown area. Building owners gave to the city the front walls of their buildings. The city removed inappropriate metal, plastic, or tile coverings to make the fronts of the buildings look as they had when they had been built. The owners were required to spend an equal amount of money to improve the interiors of their buildings in exchange for the exterior work. This arrangement was called the Façade Easement Program and it became a national model, studied and emulated by cities around the country.

The federal government provided money to redesign Cherry Street. Sidewalks were rebuilt, trees planted, new lights added, and parking meters removed. Downtown became a more pleasant place to walk and drive, to shop and work.

Downtown was a better place to be, but it needed people. Several ideas were tried to urge people to live downtown. Owners created apartments in unused second floors of their buildings. A government project removed buildings in poor condition and replaced them with new apartments. The old Dempsey Hotel was made into apartments for the elderly. In the nearby areas more than one hundred old houses were restored and occupied.

By the end of the twentieth century downtown was alive but still struggling. The original planned part of Macon had seen cotton wagons, slave auctions, invading armies, gas buggies, victory celebrations, bank panics, military parades, and much more Macon history. How would it endure to witness history yet to be made?

❖

Peyton T. Anderson was the last local publisher of "The Macon Telegraph". He committed his life to serving his community and continues to serve in significant ways after his death. The Peyton Anderson Foundation provides money for countless worthwhile projects in Macon.

Chapter VI

Into the New Millenium

As Macon entered the twenty-first century the city faced daunting challenges. Companies such as the Insurance Company of North America, Charter Medical, and Brown and Williamson were relocated. The population, which had stood at more than 122,000 in 1970, had declined to slightly more than 97,000 in 2000. As surrounding counties grew steadily Bibb grew slowly as the city lost population. This decline reflected a nationwide trend of urban centers losing population to surrounding areas, a trend referred to as "sprawl". In spite of late-twentieth-century efforts to halt the flight to the suburbs the trend continued. Recognizing the threat, a coalition of business, institutional, and government leaders united to counteract the trend. They formed Newtown Macon, an organization named for the original settlement at Fort Hawkins. Drawing funding from many sources the coalition was dedicated to revitalizing the central city. A major resource was the Peyton Anderson Foundation, a charitable agency created by the bequest of the last private and local owners of the *Macon Telegraph*. Using subsidies, grants, political influence, and powers of persuasion Newtown Macon has been able to produce results. New businesses

The Macon Coliseum was designed to suggest an Indian Mound. When it was built in the 1960s "urban renewal" was considered a good thing. An entire historic neighborhood of East Macon was removed in order to accommodate the building and its acres of parking.

The Coliseum was expanded with convention facilities and became the Centreplex.

have been recruited to locate downtown and downtown living has been encouraged by the development of a wealth of lofts in previously unused spaces. Perhaps Newtown Macon's most visible success has been the development of the Ocmulgee Trail, a river walk making the riverfront accessible to the public for the first time in over a century. A playground, parks and miles of walking trails have attracted thousands to the ancient sacred river banks.

Another reason for optimism about Macon's future is a growing emphasis on and support for tourism. A clean industry which benefits the community as a whole, tourism is a natural for Macon with its rich history and outstanding architecture. At the foot of Cherry Street a restored Terminal Station, once the hub of Macon's railroad activity, is now anchor for Macon's museum district. The state sponsored Georgia Music Hall of Fame and Georgia Sports Hall of Fame are in close proximity to the new home of the Tubman African-American Museum and the Children's Museum. Add to these a vibrant downtown nightlife offering a wide variety of restaurants, clubs, and theatres and live music to suit almost any taste and Macon is becoming a magnet for visitors.

And, so, despite difficulties, risks and challenges Macon approaches its two-hundredth birthday with reasons to look forward to a bright future. Its assets have not changed. Its excellent location in the heart of the state makes it a transportation crossroads. It remains a commercial and cultural center for its region. And its greatest asset is still its citizenry, people of vision, imagination and determination. They have steered the old town through calamities large and small. Their spiritual descendants, today's citizens, who love their hometown, will work to ensure its continued success well into its third century.

Left: The Ocmulgee Heritage Trail provides miles of walking trails and is entered at one point beside the Otis Redding Memorial Bridge at Gateway Park.

Below: The Macon-Bibb County Convention and Visitors Bureau is a logical first stop for people visiting Macon. It is housed in a former bus station where music great Little Richard was once a dishwasher.

60 ✦ HISTORIC MACON

Opposite, top: A row of once derelict historic buildings on lower Poplar Street has been renovated and overlooks a redesigned median meant to represent "Macon's backyard".

Opposite, bottom: In 1968 Macon Junior College was established on a large campus west of town. Its student population has mushroomed since it was expanded to four year status and re-named Macon State College.

Left: The Johnston-Felton-Hay House is an 1859 Italian Renaissance villa built by William Butler Johnston, Macon Comptroller for the Confederacy. Its technological innovations, including three original bathrooms with hot and cold running water, made it a technological marvel for its time. Today it is owned by the Georgia Trust for Historic Preservation and is one of the city's foremost attractions.

BIBLIOGRAPHY

PUBLISHED SOURCES

Akers, Samuel Luttrell. *The First Hundred Years of Wesleyan College*. Macon, Georgia: The Stinehour Press, 1976.

Anderson, Nancy Briska. *Macon: A Pictorial History*. Virginia Beach, Virginia: Donning Company Publishers, 1979.

Andrews, Eliza Frances. *The War-Time Journal of a Georgia Girl*. Macon, Georgia: The Ardivan Press, 1960.

Butler, John C. *The Alexander Free School: The Life of Elam Alexander*. Macon, Georgia: J. W. Burke Company, 1886.

Butler, John C. *Historical Record of Macon and Central Georgia*. Macon, Georgia: J. W. Burke Company, 1879; reprinted Macon, Georgia: The Middle Georgia Historical Society, 1969.

Coulter, E. Merton. *A Short History of Georgia*. Chapel Hill, North Carolina: The University of North Carolina Press, 1933. pp. 207, 240, 242-248, 265, 304, 335, 382-3, 408.

D'Antignac, Munroe. "Simri Rose, *The Telegraph*'s Father." *The Georgia Magazine of the Macon Telegraph*, January 31, 1943. pp. 1-6.

Dowell, Spright. *A History of Mercer University, 1883-1953*. Atlanta, Georgia: Foote and Davies, Inc., 1958.

Fisk, H. F. C. "Jerry Cowles", *Genealogy of the Cowles Family in America*. New Haven, Connecticut: Tuttle, Morehouse, and Taylor Company, 1929. pp. 706-708.

Flanders, R. B., "Ambrose Baber", "The Georgia Historical Quarterly", XII, 3, September, 1938, pp. 209-248.

Harris, Nathaniel E. *Autobiography: The Story of an Old Man's Life With Reminiscences of Seventy-Five Years*. Macon, Georgia: J. W. Burke Company, 1925.

Harris, General Walter A. *Here the Creeks Sat Down*. Macon, Georgia: J. W. Burke Company, 1958.

Iobst, Richard W. *Civil War Macon*. Macon, Georgia: Mercer University Press, 1999.

Jones, Mary Callaway. "Cowles' Mansion House." *The Macon Telegraph and News Magazine*, November 9, 1930. pp. 1-4.

Lamar, Dolly Blount. *When All is Said and Done*. Athens, Georgia: University of Georgia Press, 1952.

Loyles, Thomas W. *Georgia's Public Men*. Atlanta, Georgia: Byrd Printing Co., 1902. pp. 6-8.

Macon and the Ocmulgee National Monument, Workers of the Writers' Program of the Works Projects Administration, Macon, GA: J. W. Burke Co., 1939.

The Macon News, Hundredth Anniversary Edition, July 10, 1929.

"Macon Meets Responsibilities of Teeming Wartime Populace." *The Macon Telegraph*, August 29, 1944. p. 2A.

The Macon Telegraph and News, Sesquicentennial Edition, September 28, 1973.

McKay, John J., editor. *A Guide to Macon's Architectural and Historical Heritage*. Macon, Georgia: The Middle Georgia Historical Society, 1972.

McSwain, Eleanor Davis. *The Founding Fathers of the County of Bibb and the Town of Macon, Georgia, 1823*. Macon, Georgia: National Printing Company, 1977.

Meeks, Catherine. *Macon's Black Heritage: The Untold Story*. Macon, GA: Tubman African-American Museum, 1997.

Nirenstein, Virginia King. *With Kindly Voices: A Nineteenth Century Georgia Family*. Macon, Georgia: Tullous Books, 1984.

Northen, William T., editor. *Men of Mark in Georgia*, volume 3. Atlanta, Georgia: A. B. Caldwell, Publisher, 1911. pp. 234-237, 530-533, 566-581.

Pope, G. D., Jr. "Ocmulgee National Monument, Georgia." *National Parks Service Handbook 24*. Washington, D.C.: United States Department of the Interior, 1956.

Simms, Kristina. *Macon: Georgia's Central City*. Chatsworth, California: Windsor Publications, Inc., 1989.

Sparks, George, editor. *Macon's War Work: A History of Macon's Part in The Great World War*. Macon, Georgia: J. W. Burke Company, 1918.

Wylie, Lollie Belle, editor. *Memoirs of Judge Richard H. Clark*. Atlanta, Georgia: Franklin Printing Company, 1898. pp. 27-43.

Young, Ida, Julius Gholson, and Clara Nell Hargrove. *The History of Macon, Georgia*. Macon, Georgia: Lyon, Marshall, and Brooks Press, 1950.

UNPUBLISHED SOURCES

Anderson, George David, "A City Comes of Age: An Urban Study of Macon, Georgia During the 1920s", Master's Thesis, Georgia College, Milledgeville, Georgia, August, 1975.

Harris, General Walter A., "Elam Alexander, The Builder" in "Some Paper Given at the Palaver Club by General Walter A. Harris", Caroline Hazlehurst Harrell, editor, 1978.

Hawkins, Benjamin, "A Sketch of the Creek Country in the Years 1798-1799", in the collections of the Georgia Historical Society, Savannah, Georgia, 1916.

Intown Historic District Preservation Plan Update, Urban Design Consultants, Inc., Community Development, City of Macon, Georgia, 1983.

Jenkins, William Thomas, "Ante Bellum Macon and Bibb County, Georgia", Doctoral Dissertation, University of Georgia, Athens, Georgia, 1966.

Koch, Mary Levin, "A History of the Arts in Augusta, Macon, and Columbus, Georgia, 1800-1806", Master's Thesis, University of Georgia, Athens, Georgia, 1983.

"Macon Facts and Information", City of Macon, Georgia, 1985.

McInvale, Morton, "Macon and the Civil War", Master's Thesis, Florida State University, Tallahassee, Florida, 1973.

Minutes of City Council, January 1939-October 1943, City of Macon, Georgia. pp. 529-700.

Minutes of City Council, November 1943-December 1947, City of Macon, Georgia. pp. 1-203.

Papin, Fanny Lockett, Letter to Mary Callaway Jones, 1949, Overlook House File, Genealogical and Historical Room, Middle Georgia Regional Library.

Rose, Simri, "A Diary Journal of Simri Rose, 1830", Hermione Ross Walker, Editor, Unpublished Manuscript, Genealogical and Historical Room, Middle Georgia Regional Library.

Ross, Edgar A., "Reminiscences of Simri Rose", manuscript dated May 24, 1924, Genealogical and Historical Room, Middle Georgia Regional Library.

"We Too Built America: Recovering the American Heritage of Three Ethnic / Minority Groups in the Middle Georgia Area", Handbook produced by the Bibb County Public Schools and the Booker T. Washington Community Center, Macon, Georgia, 1981-82.

Sharing the Heritage

historic profiles of businesses, organizations, and families that have contributed to the development and economic base of Macon

Atlantic Southern Bank	66
Nu-Way Weiners	70
Anderson, Walker & Reichert, LLP	72
Smith & Sons Foods	74
River Edge Behavioral Health Center	76
Macon Water Authority	78
Jean and Hall Florists	80
Mount de Sales Academy	82
Historic Macon Foundation	84
Fore(In)Sight Foundation	86
1842 Inn	87
Wesleyan College	88
Macon-Bibb County Transit Authority	89
Jones, Cork & Miller, LLP	90
GEICO	91
Truan Sales, Inc.	92
Carlyle Place	93
Macon Sewing Center	94
Hays Service, LLC	95
Macon Convention & Visitors Bureau	96
Parks & Roberts Tax Service	97
Broadway Lofts	98
A. T. Long & Son Painting	99
Pilot International	100
Macon Centreplex	101
Mercer University	102
Medical Center of Central Georgia	103
Coldwell Banker SSK	104
Georgia Power	105

Special Thanks to

Ship & Shore Travel Agency

Atlantic Southern Bank

❖

Above: Lori Poarch, Tammy Blann, Mark Stevens and Carol Soto celebrate the groundbreaking for the two-story main branch on Forsyth Road in Macon, February 2002.

Below: Board members joining the bank staff members for the ribbon cutting at the first branch of New Southern Bank, December 10, 2001.

In 2000, shortly after leaving his job as president of a local regional bank, Mark Stevens began work on an idea that had been germinating in his mind for some time. It was to create a new community bank for a fast growing, diversified Macon economy. That was the genesis of Atlantic Southern Bank.

Realizing running a bank is one thing, but starting one from scratch is quite another, which would have a significant impact on not only his business career but also his family life, Stevens had serious talks about the venture with his wife, Deborah. He then had lengthy discussions with Georgia Banking Commissioner Steve Bridges. Next, he met with Carol Soto, a long-time associate with extensive banking experience as a chief financial officer, to get her feedback.

All agreed the time was right for a new community bank in Macon and that he had the experience and leadership ability to lead the effort.

Soto, who was instrumental in organizing the new bank, recalls, "The organizational period was a very exciting time. The minimum level of capital that had to be raised was $7.5 million. The capital campaign ended on November 9 and $8 million was raised in just ninety-nine days."

Soto recounts how in a short time, "We opened on December 10, 2001, in a double wide modular unit on Forsyth Road. Within the first ninety days, three more team members were added: Brandon Mercer was brought on as a Commercial Lender, Annie Reed was hired as a Lending Assistant, and Gail Davis became the bank's first credit analyst. The months in the modular unit were a time of bonding and building of lasting relationships among each other as we were in very close quarters! Construction on the permanent facility began in February 2002, and the building was completed in late August. We all had mixed emotions when it came time to move to the new building. While we were excited about our beautiful new bank building with all the extra space, we were sad that the closeness was changing. It was not long, however, before we were able to add new employees and soon the new building was fully occupied."

When informed of the project, Gary Hall, a family friend of many years, expressed excitement about the prospects for a new community bank and offered to lend his expertise as a chief credit officer to the effort. "Previously Mark and I both worked for independent community banks that were merged into large holding companies….He asked if I would have any interest in working in community banking again. Naturally, I said 'yes'. Within a short period of time, the bank was becoming a reality and he asked if I would consider joining the team. I immediately answered 'yes' and was honored to be included," he remembers.

The bank got a divine boost when he and his long-time friend, spiritual adviser, and fellow Exchange Club member Dr. Rick Lanford, prominent Macon minister, were working at the Georgia State Fair. Dr. Lanford was impressed with his friend's bank idea and suggested saying a prayer on its behalf. It must have worked because Dr. Lanford was among the initial investors and influenced several of his friends to join the team.

Dr. Lanford commented on his meeting at the State Fair with Mark and Deborah: "Mark indicated he'd talked to others about starting a new community bank. I recall joining hands with them and praying for God's wisdom to guide our thoughts and actions in bringing this vision of a new bank to reality."

Among those who followed Dr. Lanford's guidance to become backers of the bank were Dr. Trip Smisson, Russell Lipford, and Pete Cates. George Waters and Carl Hofstadter accepted Cates' invitation to be among the original investors.

Above: Chairman of the Board Bill Fickling III looks on as President and CEO Mark Stevens speaks on the opening day of the modular branch on Forsyth in Macon on December 10, 2001.

Below: Main branch near completion summer of 2002.

Meanwhile several of Stevens' other long-time friends, Rob Ballard, Carolyn Crayton, T.J. Rauls, Doug Dunwody, and Tom McMichael agreed with his assessment that it was time to have a dynamic, new financial institution to serve Central Georgia's increasing banking needs.

"Although I am a very optimist thinker, I never expected a new bank to impact the lives of so many people. Assembling a talented group of individuals that didn't know each other and creating an environment with everyone working for a common purpose and goal and to provide opportunities for their development is the fun part and most rewarding," Stevens said.

The bank gained further credibility when at an organizational meeting William "Bill" Fickling III, one of Macon's most prominent business and civic leaders, agreed to be chairman. Stevens first met Fickling over lunch to discuss a potential new bank charter.

The founding group received approval for a new bank charter from the Georgia Department of Banking and Finance and raised initial capital of $8.5 million in a record 99 days, signaling the confidence of the community. Today the bank has more than $825 million in assets with fifteen branches in eight Georgia counties.

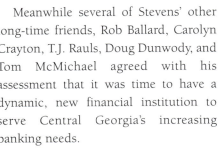

Right: Governor Sonny Perdue speaks with the media about the opening of the new branch and corporate center.

Below: Chairman of the Board Bill Fickling, III welcomes Governor Sonny Perdue as Atlantic Southern Bank opens the new corporate center, North Winds, September 6, 2007.

Atlantic Southern now employs 170 and has added Donald Moore from Savannah and Mike Griffin of Macon as directors of the holding company.

Organized in 2001 as New South Bank and later named New Southern, the bank became Atlantic Southern Bank in 2005 when it entered the Savannah market. With the purchase of Sapelo National Bank in 2006 Atlantic Southern moved into the Darien, Brunswick, and St. Simons Island market. The Valdosta Loan Production office opened in 2007. That same year Atlantic Southern stock first traded on NASDAQ under the symbol ASFN.

In its short but storied six year history, Atlantic Southern has moved forward showing controlled growth and steady progress and now has five operating regions.

The Central Georgia Region currently is made up of the Macon branches, Lizella and Roberta. Warner Robins, Bonaire, and Byron makes up the Mid-South Region. The Coastal Region branches are Savannah and Rincon. A branch will open soon in fast growing Pooler.

Due to a name conflict with another banking institution the Golden Isles Region operates under the name Sapelo Southern Bank and has branches in Brunswick, Darien, and St. Simons Island. Valdosta, just north of the Florida line, comprises the South Region with a new branch slated to open in 2008. These five regions allow Atlantic Southern to provide efficient and convenient banking services to a wide range of customers.

In August 2007 the Bank opened its Corporate Center, known as North Winds, in Macon. The Operations Center for ASB is also located in Macon.

In a move to provide its services to one of the nation's fastest growing and most diverse markets, the bank purchased a charter to operate in Florida in 2007, paving the road to an even brighter future for Atlantic Southern.

The bank reached a milestone on September 6, 2007, when Georgia Governor Sonny Perdue, a central Georgia native, spoke at the ribbon cutting and dedication of the modern new North Winds Corporate Center. The Governor commented on how the addition of North Winds in north Bibb County aids the development of this increasingly important part of Macon—Bibb. He also remarked on how the history of bank founder Mark Stevens and his family is intertwined with the civic progress and religious life of the area when he talked about the late Dr. Jimmy Waters, prominent Macon minister, who was Stevens' father-in-law. Coincidently, the I-75 interchange where the Center is located is named in honor of Dr. Waters.

The new Corporate Center is the latest concrete example of the continuing forward progress of Atlantic Southern.

❖

Above: Governor Perdue addresses directors, officers, employees and other special friends at the North Winds ribbon cutting.

Below: A celebration among the North Winds employees as Governor Perdue and President/CEO Mark Stevens cuts the ribbon.

Nu-Way Weiners

Swivel-top barstools and chrome-trimmed countertops, first-name familiarities exchanged between patrons and staff, the heady aroma of grilled meat and simmering chili: this is Nu-Way Weiners, the quintessential Macon experience. For ninety-two years, Nu-Way has been a mainstay of the city's existence, an important part of which is noshing, grabbing lunch, or indulging in a hearty dinner. Nu-Way's appeal bridges geographic distances and cultural gaps, appealing to Southerners and Yanks alike, to low-brow chowhounds and gourmands both.

Gourmet Magazine cited Nu-Way as "one of America's ten best hot dog joints," while *The Macon Telegraph* notes the supremacy of the restaurant's sweet tea. And Lewis Grizzard and *The New York Times* agree about one thing, if nothing else: Nu-Way is among the best in its class. Only a taste of the highest quality could unite such disparate elements of culture and geography.

The signature beef-and-pork hot dog and spicy chili captivates the taste buds of Central Georgians and non-natives alike. The bright red wieners are made uniquely to Nu-Way specifications, and the chili is made from scratch, using the original recipe. The house specialty is a hot dog on a bun steamed to a warm, tender perfection and topped with hot chili sauce and cole slaw, with condiments to taste. Crispy fries are the perfect accompaniment, and no Nu-Way meal is complete without a fountain drink or sweet tea over Famous Flaky Ice. Burger lovers will be satisfied with the Mega-Burger, "A Meal in Itself." Plus Nu-Way serves fresh hot breakfasts, including biscuits, bacon and eggs.

Launched by Greek immigrant James Mallis in 1916, the original Nu-Way was housed inside a grocery store on Cotton Avenue. In the 1930s, by a fluke, the name picked up the idiosyncratic spelling of wieners: A sign painter misspelled the name as Nu-Way Weiners. The owners at the time fancied it bad luck to change the spelling once the job was complete, so the quirky spelling remained. And the store has been Nu-Way Weiners ever since. Nu-Way's development has mirrored that of the city, expanding from its original downtown location to eleven locations in Central Georgia.

Many Nu-Way patrons are part of a long lineage of Nu-Way lovers. For some families, visiting the restaurant is a tradition and part of what makes Macon unique. And just as patronizing Nu-Way is a multi-generational activity, so is working for Nu-Way. Nu-Way enjoys having third- and fourth-generation employees, some of whom have worked for the business for

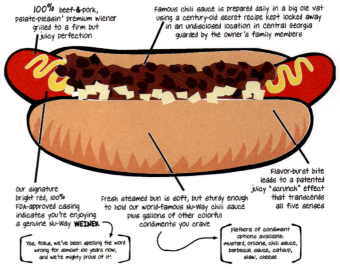

more than thirty years. From its inception, the restaurant aspired to cultivate a team of dedicated employees through training and development. These efforts have helped to establish the family atmosphere the restaurants are known for.

Co-owners and cousins Jim Cacavias and Spyros Dermatas are third-generation owners in what continues to be a closely-held family business. The two bring unusual credentials to a family-owned restaurant chain. Both Georgia Tech graduates, they hold fast to the original values established by their great-uncle and founder: quality, service, cleanliness, and value. Melded with the respect they have for Nu-Way's tradition is the ethic to continually improve and adapt to changing needs, tastes, and lifestyles. Nu-Way has supplemented its traditional menu offerings with choices to accommodate health-conscious diners, and value packages give customers convenient options. Nu-Way's catering service also provides food for events from small gatherings to grand celebrations. Nu-Way has evolved with the times, yet continues to embody the ineffable quality that is Nu-Way.

In spite of its modest, no-frills approach to cooking up the perfect meal, Nu-Way has enjoyed acclaim from a host of media sources. In addition to the previously mentioned accolades, Nu-Way has been featured in *Money Magazine*, *Southern Living*, and in Southern food guru John T. Edge's compendium of top eats, *Southern Belly*. The hot dog joint has also received television coverage from *Travel Channel* and *The Today Show*. And it was featured prominently in a 1999 PBS documentary, *A Hot Dog Program*, which highlighted the most notable hot dogs in the U.S.

Even with the effusive praise it has received over the years, Nu-Way stays true to its course: serving tasty, high-quality meals quickly and with courteous service. And that is what makes Nu-Way a cornerstone of Macon's culture.

ANDERSON, WALKER & REICHERT, LLP

There is a historic relationship between the law firm of Anderson, Walker and Reichert and the city of Macon, deeply rooted in cultural and educational contributions and public service. Anderson, Walker and Reichert's stated primary mission is "rendering excellent legal services to clients" which includes representing clients in court as well as keeping them out of court. That philosophy, accompanied by a strong emphasis on integrity and community betterment, has been the tradition in a law practice spanning three centuries. Honoring this heritage, lawyers at Anderson, Walker & Reichert consider law a profession, not a business. Meeting clients' needs is their primary reward: getting paid to do so is a bonus.

The original letterhead for Lanier & Anderson, the precursor to today's Anderson, Walker & Reichert.

The firm traces its origins to 1849 when Robert Sampson Lanier and his brother-in-law William Henry Anderson began practicing law together in the growing and prosperous city of Macon. Lanier was born in Athens after his father moved from North Carolina to establish hotels along the burgeoning southern frontier, among them Macon's Lanier House. Lanier met Anderson in college in Virginia and married Anderson's sister Mary Jane in 1840. In 1842, they became parents of the poet and musician Sidney Lanier. A much younger brother, Clifford Anderson came to Macon to be close to his kin after being orphaned and left penniless in 1845. Undaunted by his circumstances, the youngster educated himself by reading the classics, and then law, while working at the Lanier family's downtown hotel.

Formal legal education was rare in those days. Aspiring lawyers trained in the offices of other lawyers, reading law books and observing the practice of their mentors. They were required to appear before a Superior Court judge for "examination;" if they passed, they were admitted to the bar. William Henry Anderson died unexpectedly at twenty-eight; nevertheless Clifford continued to study under Robert Lanier; was admitted to the bar in 1852 at age nineteen, and immediately joined Lanier's practice, known then and for many years after as "Lanier and Anderson." Age difference was never a problem. The two men had complementary talents and were admired for industry, amiability, intellect, and probity. In an era when lawyers tended to practice alone or to change partners frequently, only Lanier's death in 1893 ended their remarkable partnership.

The firm's involvement in public service got off to an early start in 1856 when Clifford was named judge of the newly established City Court of Macon. After serving a year he recommended that it be abolished. Subsequently, he was elected to the Macon City Council, and later to the state legislature and Confederate Congress. He was Georgia's Attorney General from 1880-1890, earning praise from notables like former governor Nat Harris who described him as "probably the ablest, and on many accounts the most remarkable practitioner before the bar at this time in the state." When Mercer established a law school in 1878, Anderson became a

ANDERSON, WALKER & REICHERT
THROUGH 158 YEARS OF MACON HISTORY

Lanier & Anderson 1849	Anderson & Grace 1899	Anderson & Anderson 1937
Lanier, Anderson & Anderson 1891	Ryals, Grace & Anderson 1909	Anderson, Anderson & Walker 1941
Anderson & Anderson 1893	Ryals & Anderson 1912	Anderson, Anderson, Walker & Reichert 1953
Anderson, Anderson & Grace 1897	Ryals, Anderson & Anderson 1925	Anderson, Walker & Reichert 1959

member of its first faculty, beginning a close relationship between the university and the firm that continued into the twentieth century when the school's first building was named for partner T. E. Ryals in recognition of his efforts in its constuction. Over the years, several members of the firm have taught law at Mercer.

Most of Lanier's and Anderson's sons followed their fathers into the practice of law, although most left Macon in the lean years after the Civil War. One lawyer became more famous as a poet. Sidney Lanier, after several years of practicing law, found the lure of music and poetry irresistible, and followed his muse north to Baltimore. Anderson's eldest practiced for a time in Macon before moving to Atlanta, where he founded the firm of Anderson and Rountree, known for most of the twentieth century as Hansell and Post. Another son, James, practiced with his father and uncle for about fifteen years before heading to Atlanta after his brother's first law partner had died.

It was left to the sixth son to carry on the old firm. In 1871, Anderson had notified his partner of the child's arrival with a trace of humor:

> Dear Bro. Robert, Another boy baby born this morning about 9 o'clock. I suppose I shall have to name him "Smith." Please send letters & papers and arrange, if you can, for law class at 4 this p.m. Am sleepy and tired; will try to go down tomorrow. Annie and baby doing well. Aff., C. A.

Instead of Smith, the child was christened Robert Lanier Anderson and he became the link tying the nineteenth century firm to today's. Admitted to the bar in 1893 in time to help his father complete the monumental 1895 annotation of the Georgia Code, this Anderson formed a thirty-year partnership with Thomas Edward Ryals; his son, Robert Lanier Anderson, Jr., joined them in 1922 and Charles W. Walker in 1933. During the Depression, Ryals left the firm. Albert P. Reichert joined in 1949. The firm took its present name in 1959 after the death of the elder Anderson. Current partners are Thomas L. Bass, Albert P. Reichert, Jr., Eugene S. Hatcher, Robert A. B. Reichert, and Jonathan A. Alderman. Albert P. Reichert remains of counsel.

The practice of law has changed as Macon and the area's business community have grown and become more complex, but Anderson, Walker & Reichert's adherence to the highest ethical standards, devotion to public service, and the collegiality of their practice has remained constant and steadfast. In response to changes, the firm has broadened its service abilities and remains committed to continuing education, keeping the firm well ahead of changes in the legal profession and justice system. Like most lawyers today, members specialize in various aspects of law in order better to meet the needs of their business and individual clients.

Good "lawyering" requires hard work supported by creativity and imagination to reach optimal solutions. The firm operates on the premise that planning is the key: foresight avoids disputes while serving client interests. Should a dispute arise, or reasonable settlement becomes impossible, prevailing in court becomes the goal.

Anderson, Walker & Reichert, LLP participates in trials in all courts and practices in the following areas: general practice, corporation, insurance defense, tax, estates and trusts, wills, probate, real estate, environmental, bankruptcy, employment, and family law, including adoptions.

(From left to right) Albert P. Reichert, R. Lanier Anderson, Jr., and Charles W. Walker, whose names still identify Macon's oldest law firm, are shown here on the occasion of Anderson's fiftieth year of practice. Both Walker and Reichert also practiced with the firm for over fifty years.

Sharing the Heritage ✦ 73

Smith & Sons Foods

Smith & Sons Foods, a Macon institution for over seven decades, was founded in 1936 by the late J. A. Smith, Jr., who was a pioneer in integrating retail and wholesale food services, marrying S&S Cafeterias, S&S Food Administrators and State Wholesale Food to create today's company, which provides one of the highest levels of quality food and distribution services in the restaurant business.

Smith, who died in 2001 at age ninety-nine, was one of the last turn-of-the-century self-made Southern entrepreneurs. He began his storybook career at the improbable age of fourteen, running a taxi service back in an era when it was possible for one so young to engage in such an endeavor. Working at various lunch counters, he was attracted to the food business and displayed an uncanny knack for seeing the future in the food business. By age twenty-five, he had been in the restaurant business in places as far away as Miami. It was in 1936 when he was thirty-four that "Smitty" founded the first S&S Cafeteria, introducing a new food service concept to the Southeast. He continued to be active in the business long after his retirement, serving as chairman of the Board Emeritus of the company until his death.

The first S&S Cafeterias in Macon were located on Cherry Street, Third Street, and Walnut Street. The Cherry Street cafeteria was a fixture in downtown Macon for forty-four years when it closed in 1984. At the same time Cherry Street closed, the Bloomfield Village cafeteria opened across from the Macon Mall. The Third Street cafeteria opened in 1946 and closed in 1961 when the Walnut Street location opened. (Walnut Street closed in 1975.) In addition to the Bloomfield Village cafeteria, the Riverside Drive location has been serving loyal customers since its opening in October 1972.

Not only was Smith a leading businessman in Macon and the Southeast, he was a civic leader with a deep Christian faith. He was encouraged and supported throughout his business life by his devoted Christian wife, Marguerite, who died in 1986.

The Smith legacy is continued today by family members and key employees who are making major contributions to the future of the company. One of the early key executives was Vice President/Secretary/Treasurer Clarence Johnson, who served the company for fifty-five years until his death in March 1990. He put into place financial policies and guidelines which have been instrumental in the stability and progress of Smith & Sons Foods over the years.

Smith family members continue to lead the company following in their father and grandfather's footsteps:
- President and CEO James A. Smith III;
- Executive Vice President Robert A. Smith;

Above: J. R. Smith, R. A. Smith, J. A. Smith, III, and J. A. Smith, IV.

Below: J. A. Smith V prepares to open the serving line at the Riverside Drive Cafeteria.

- Vice President of Cafeteria Operations James A. Smith IV;
- District Manager Judson R. Smith;
- Two great grandsons of founder; David Smith and J.A. Smith V, are in management and being groomed for future roles in leadership of the company; and
- Vice President of Food Administrators R. A. Smith Jr., also a grandson of the founder, passed away in March 2005.

Other key personnel helping lead Smith & Sons Foods into the future include:

- Senior Vice President of Operations and Administration Ralph M. Bennett;
- Vice President/Secretary/Treasurer Randall E. Douthit;
- Controller David R. Johnson;
- Director of Human Resources Melissa C. Smith;
- District Manager of the cafeteria division Louis R. Bennett III;
- Divisional Vice President of Food Administrators Grant L. Bennett;
- General Manager Raylon A. Soles directs the commissary State Wholesale Food;
- Assured Quality Control Corporate Representative Joseph G. Kight; and
- Director of Advertising Rita W. Kiser.

S&S Cafeterias are noted for the quality and variety of their food and the attentiveness of their service. Smith family recipes, handed down through generations, such as Macaroni and Cheese, Chicken and Dumplings, Chicken Pan Pie, Country Fried Steak, Egg Custard Pie and Chess Pie, are among some of the signature dishes.

S&S Cafeterias presently has locations in Atlanta, Augusta, and Macon, Georgia; North Augusta, Charleston, Columbia, and Greenville, South Carolina; and Knoxville, Tennessee. The Corporate Office is located on Riverside Drive in Macon.

The creation in 1949 of State Wholesale Food, the purchasing arm of the company, has assured the highest quality ingredients for the most efficient cost. Today, this division operates out of a modern warehouse/distribution hub centrally located. As a part of this distribution center, State Wholesale Food also maintains a USDA inspected food processing department, which assists all of the units in their efforts to offer its customers quality food on a consistent basis. This department is led by Director of Food Processing Jerry Evans. Other key employees are Director of Purchasing Lora Darmohray and Warehouse Manager Orrin Carstarphen.

Smith & Sons Foods again set a standard for the industry in 1957 when S&S Food Administrators was created. This arm of the company provides food service management to hospitals, nursing homes, industries, and educational accounts. Efficiencies in the area of dietary healthcare needs also have been expanded. Assisting Grant Bennett is Director of Business Development Ed Larsen. He is responsible for developing contacts to secure new accounts for this division. Serving as District Managers are Gene LeRoy, Mike McCasland, and Susie Stansbery.

Throughout these seventy plus years, S&S has continued to provide the highest quality food services for the best value.

"No matter how technology and business trends change, our commitment to quality and conservative business concepts will keep Smith & Sons Foods a vital and prosperous food service company as we continue to serve our community and customers in the future," commented President/CEO James A. Smith III.

Above: S&S Cafeteria located on Riverside Drive in Macon.

Below: An aerial view of State Wholesale Food.

River Edge Behavioral Health Center

River Edge Behavioral Health Center (REBHC) began in 1950 as the Child Guidance Center of the Macon-Bibb Health Department and has evolved into a leader in behavioral healthcare, providing comprehensive services for seven middle Georgia Counties.

The River Edge Behavioral Health Community Service Board serves residents of Baldwin, Bibb, Jones, Monroe, Putnam, Twiggs, and Wilkinson counties, offering high quality treatment for persons with mental illness, psychological disorders, addictive disease, or developmental disabilities.

The history of River Edge mirrors the progression of comprehensive mental health services in the state. In 1959 the local health department added public health nursing services to families of patients with mental illness returning to the community from Georgia's Central State Hospital in Milledgeville.

By 1961, Bibb, Jones, and Twiggs County health departments pooled their resources to form the first multi-county mental health program in the state. The continuum of available mental health services included outpatient psychiatric services for youth and adults, mental health education and consultation for professionals.

In 1970, with the increase in drug use, a drug rehabilitation program was initiated and staffed by college students. The next year the Central Georgia Comprehensive Community Mental Health, Mental Retardation and Substance Abuse Center was formed under the director of the Bibb County Board of Health. Monroe County was added to the service area in 1991.

There was a seminal moment in the history of mental health in Georgia when state law was changed in 1993. This law allowed the development and governance for mental health, addictive disease and developmental disabilities services by an independent board of county-appointed community leaders, service consumers and their families from each of the served counties. The first governance board was formed in 1994 with nine members.

The organization was named River Edge Behavioral Health Center in 1995 to reflect the new level of ownership among the many communities it serves and its main office is located on the edge of the historic Ocmulgee River in Macon.

River Edge annually provides a comprehensive array of community-based services delivering hope, recovery, and independence for more than 8,000 child, teen, and adult members of the seven county areas with severe mental illness, severe emotional disturbance, addictive disease, or developmental disabilities. The organization is the most comprehensive and stable community provider of community-based mental health, developmental disability, and addictive disease treatment, and support services in the region.

Above: River Edge Community Service Board, left to right: Mattie Middlebrooks, Myrtice Vinson, Vice Chair Bill Willingham, Elmo Richardson, Andy Galloway, Chair Ray Bennett and Secretary Oreatha Sewell.

Below: A doctor visit.

Adult mental health and addictive services include:
- Case management with individual community support and case management outreach;
- Outpatient clinical services including crisis intervention, psychiatric care and medical stabilization, individual family and group counseling, and medical maintenance;
- Clinical day services with group training, training for success, psychosocial rehabilitation, and peer supports;
- Supported housing services including crisis group home, transitional housing and shelter plus care and supported living arrangements; and
- Hospitalization (not provided by REBHC) crisis stabilization unit and residential detox.

For adults with a developmental disability, River Edge offers:
- Day Habilitation: Structured supports to decrease maladaptive behaviors, teach basic communication, activities of daily living, adaptive community living and leisure skills, improve social, emotional, and intellectual development.
- Day Supports: Structured supports focused on pre-vocational skill development, community inclusion through volunteer opportunities and supported employment.
- Supported Employment: Competitive market job placement, coaching and support.
- Residential/Housing Services: Community living opportunities in own home or natural/family caregiver's home.
- Respite: Support to the caregivers of persons with mental retardation (NOTE: This service available for individuals' age three years and older.)
- Natural Support Enhancement: Individualized assistance to caregivers to foster the person with mental retardation remaining in the natural/family caregiver's home.

River Edge services for adults with mental retardation/co-occurring disorders offers basically the same services in the above adult mental health and addictive services category.

River Edge is a member of the Chamber of Commerce in each of the counties it serves. It conducts an annual Adopt a Foster Child for Christmas in partnership with the Bibb DFCS. River Edge locations are also Kids Yule Love collection sites. In addition, River Edge hosts annual blood drives for the American Red Cross.

Today, River Edge Behavioral Health Center has an annual budget of $22 million and serves more than 8000 clients a year with a staff of approximately 400.

River Edge's vision remains to be the keystone provider of behavioral healthcare in the community. It continues to be known throughout the state and nation for high quality work and the professionalism and excellence of its staff.

Above: River Edge Behavioral Health Center.

Below: Pharmacy visit.

Macon Water Authority

Right: Javors J. Lucas Lake is a 625-acre reservoir that can hold up to 6.5 billion gallons of raw water at full pool. It's also the site of seasonal public fishing and the annual Kids Fishing Derby in June.
COURTESY OF MARK STROZIER.

Below: The MWA Frank C. Amerson, Jr., Water Treatment Plant, with a drinking water production capacity of sixty million gallons per day, has twice been selected as the "Best Operated Plant of the Year" in Georgia.
COURTESY OF MARK STROZIER.

Of course, we all think that our part in community development is most critical, but the Macon Water Authority (MWA) and its 211 dedicated employees have a strong case for being a major contributor to the economic growth and quality of life that citizens of Macon, Bibb County, and Middle Georgia enjoy today.

Since its founding that dates back to the 1880s, the MWA has grown to serve approximately 54,000 metered water customers and more than 41,000 sewer customers in Macon and Bibb County, as well as portions of Jones and Monroe Counties, where the Authority serves as a regional wholesale water—or retail water and sewer—provider.

An elected, seven-member board of directors governs the Macon Water Authority. Five members are elected from the districts within Macon and Bibb County. The strength of this board is reflected in the experience of members such as Frank C. Amerson, Jr., the chairman who serves citizens across the county and who has thirty-one years of experience on the board. In addition, Javors J. Lucas is the Authority's Vice Chairman, with twenty-seven years of experience as the representative of District Two. Dorothy "Dot" Black is another long-standing member, representing District One, while Steve Rickman, as the newest member of the board, serves District Three, and Frank Patterson represents District Four. The final two board members—Bert Bivins, III and Ed DeFore—are selected to represent the Bibb County Commission and the Macon City Council, respectively.

The MWA board oversees an annual operating budget of approximately $41 million and net assets in excess of $220 million. In addition, the Authority is actively pursuing capital improvements and renewal and replacement of assets to maintain its water and sewer system, as well as to assure adequate infrastructure is in place for future growth.

MWA customers receive clean, safe drinking water twenty-four hours a day, seven days a week, produced at the Frank C. Amerson, Jr., Water Treatment Plant. The Amerson Plant opened July 10, 2000, replacing the Authority's Riverside Drive Water Treatment Plant, which was decommissioned followed the devastation of the 1994 flood. The new facility has a finished drinking water production capacity of 60 million gallons per day (MGD), with the ability to expand to 90 MGD in the future.

The MWA obtains its raw water for drinking water production either from Javors Lucas Lake, which is adjacent to the Amerson Plant, or directly from an intake on the Ocmulgee River. Lucas Lake is a 625-acre reservoir that can hold up to 6.5 billion gallons of water at full pool, which equates to approximately four months of reserve.

Once finished drinking water is produced at the Amerson Plant, it is stored in one of four 5 million gallon clear wells onsite. Another 15 million gallons is available thanks to seven elevated and ten ground storage tanks. MWA water is distributed to customers via approximately sixteen hundred miles of water mains and service lines. Virtually the entire water distribution system can be monitored and managed through an advanced SCADA system the Authority operates from the Amerson Plant.

Though not the most glamorous of public utility services, sewer conveyance and wastewater treatment are nonetheless critically important to quality growth in a community. Wastewater collected throughout the MWA system gravity flows or is pumped through more than nine hundred miles of sanitary sewer lines, into either the Lower Poplar or Rocky Creek Water Reclamation Facilities for treatment.

The Lower Poplar plant is an advanced secondary wastewater treatment facility with a capacity of 20 million gallons per day (MGD). The Rocky Creek facility likewise is designed to handle a monthly average flow of 24 MGD. Macon Soils—a nonprofit subsidiary established by the MWA in 1998—oversees the biosolids operations of the Authority, which includes the sale of treated material to farmers for use as fertilizer.

The measure of MWA success comes in several forms, from industry accolades to advances in customer service. All MWA facilities have received either Gold or Platinum Awards from the Georgia Association of Water Professionals (GAWP) for one hundred percent permit compliance, and the Amerson Plant has been selected twice as the Best Operated Plant of the Year in Georgia. In 2006, the MWA also won the "Collection System of the Year" Award for its sewer services. Yet within these award-winning facilities are MWA employees who have been recognized as some of the top operators, best technicians, or most outstanding public servants within the industry.

Above: The Macon Water Authority is led by a seven-member board of directors who oversee policy decisions for 211 dedicated employees, as well as 54,000 water customers and 41,000 sewer customers in Macon and Bibb County, in addition to portions of Jones and Monroe Counties.

COURTESY OF MARK STROZIER.

Below: The Macon Water Authority can store up to thirty-five million gallons of finished drinking water among its four clearwells, seven elevated tanks, and ten ground storage tanks.

COURTESY OF MARK STROZIER.

Jean and Hall Florists

Jean and Hall Florists' history is one of a family's love and dedication to each other and a business that has been a Macon institution for more than five decades.

Hall and Jean Roddenbery opened their shop in 1952 in the same two-story building on Cherry Street it still occupies. Although the couple had never before owned a business, Hall's experience dealing with people as a funeral director gave him the background and confidence to open a business which dealt with people and their needs for flowers and plants.

Until Hall's untimely death in 2007, Jean, Hall and daughters, Burney Ingle and Joy Amerson, were a team providing complete florist services to Macon and the state.

"There was always so much respect between my parents for each other," said their youngest daughter Burney. "The way they talked to one another spilled over to how they treated customers, whether long-time or new."

Commenting about how the family is carrying on with life and the business after her father's death following a long illness, Burney said, "I can't say it is not difficult. We lost the strongest link in our family chain. Throughout all these years Mom and Dad prepared Joy and me for the heart of the business and to take care of our customers. They also taught us to take care of our employees who give us great support and are our second family. We all work great together. We appreciate our customers so much because as Dad would often say, 'Without our customers … well, we just don't have a business.'"

The Roddenberys announced the grand opening for Jean and Hall on a bright, sunny day in the March 1, 1952 Sunday issue of the *Telegraph*. There was a photo of the youthful, smiling couple in each corner of the ad.

"In the beginning we were open seven days a week," Jean remembers. "We would even deliver on Christmas. There were many times I would bundle up our daughter, Joy, who was only two when we opened, and traipse off to the Dempsey

Above: Hall and Jean Roddenbery.

Hotel (a Macon landmark and its premier hotel at the time) with corsages or cut flowers. In those days we were designers, floor scrubbers, accountants, delivery people, and whatever else we had to be to make things work."

While Hall and I always hoped the girls would be interested in the business, we never pushed it on them," Jean said.

"I have always wanted to be in this business," Burney said. "I studied business at Georgia College and prepared for it. I consider myself very fortunate to work at something I truly love to do."

For a few years Joy, who also graduated from Georgia College, was an elementary school teacher, but her love for the business soon drew her back to Jean and Hall. "It wasn't long before I found myself wanting to go back to the shop," Joy said. "Our parents never pushed us to be a part of the business. Growing up, we did everything else our friends did and had a very normal childhood, but the shop held this special appeal for me. We were encouraged to help around the holidays, so I came into it with a sense of pride, having learned from my parents the importance of customer service and satisfaction."

Today, Joy and Burney are the full time operators of the business along with fourteen employees, doing everything from designing to delivery.

Jean and Hall continue to offer a wide array of services, including the services of professional designers to assist with custom designs for all occasions. In the shop's showroom there are a variety of plants, fresh fruit, gourmet items, unique gifts, stuffed animals, and Mylar balloons. Service is available for all major holidays.

Mount de Sales Academy

Above: Cavalier Field House.

In 1871 when five Sisters of Mercy arrived in Macon from nearby Columbus and opened the Academy of the Sacred Heart of Jesus, they sowed the seeds for not only the modern day Mount de Sales Academy but also the city's public school system. In 1872 the Sisters were asked to serve as founders of Bibb County's public education system, staff the school and assist in establishing the local school system. Mount de Sales, now one of the nation's top tier Catholic, independent, college prep schools, opened five years later (1876) in downtown Macon. Today, with its more than 130-year history of academic excellence within a spiritual context, Mount de Sales is widely acclaimed as a Catholic institution with a rich heritage serving students of all faiths.

The decades since those first days of Mount de Sales have brought profound changes in a school dedicated to the spiritual and intellectual growth of each student. The Academy still adheres to the principles of educating young men and women of all cultural, economic, and religious backgrounds, and continues today to provide an environment devoted to academic excellence, service to the community, global awareness, and life-long learning to meet the challenges of the twenty-first century.

Catherine McAuley, foundress of the Sisters of Mercy, handed down an axiom which students are still encouraged to follow today. She stressed "the necessity of doing extraordinarily well the ordinary actions of the day."

Several decades of dramatic growth began during the 1950s with the expansion of the campus and additional buildings. In 1959 the school became a coeducational institution at the request of the Bishop of Savannah, and the first boys entered as freshmen. In the fall of 1963, Mount de Sales became the first integrated school in Middle Georgia.

Sheridan Hall was dedicated in 1988, housing classrooms, a chapel, science and computer labs, and administrative offices. In January 1996, seventy acres of land was acquired on which the Academy's first athletic complex was completed. Cavalier Fields, the school's Dream of Fields, opened with a football stadium and practice field, soccer field and practice field, baseball field, softball field, state-

of-the-art rubberized track, tennis courts, concession house, and patio. In 2002, through the generous support of friends and families, the Academy officially completed construction of the Cavalier Field House with weightlifting and conditioning rooms, fully equipped athletic training facilities, multiple locker rooms, conference room, and coaches' offices.

The David J. Zuver Performing Arts Center, a complex where the intellectual, artistic, and aesthetic development of each student is realized, was opened in 2004. This multipurpose facility includes a 650-seat theater, practice rooms for chorus, band, and music, two art rooms, a dark room, and five classrooms.

Mount de Sales was named a National Blue Ribbon School of Excellence in 1991, the first and only private high school in Middle Georgia to receive this designation. In 2005, Mount de Sales became one of a select group of schools holding dual accreditation from both the Southern Association of Colleges and Schools and the Southern Association of Independent Schools.

The Academy continues to create an environment which encourages all students to explore opportunities designed to help develop their fullest potential. Above all, Mount de Sales challenges its faculty, staff, and students to act with integrity and to work for justice. Mount de Sales students participate in a variety of service learning, charitable, and community outreach activities including Special Olympics and Ronald McDonald House.

Present enrollment is 700 students in grades six through twelve with a faculty and staff of 92.

The main campus is located at the corner of Orange and Columbus Streets in the Intown Historic District. The Cavalier athletic complex is located on seventy acres at 4659 Cavalier Drive and on the Internet at www.mountdesales.net.

Above: The front entrance of the original high school and boarding school.

Below: David J. Zuver Performing Arts Center.

HISTORIC MACON FOUNDATION

Historic Macon Foundation, Inc. was founded in August 2003 through the merger of Macon's two leading preservation organizations, the Middle Georgia Historical Society and the Macon Heritage Foundation.

As the elder organization, the Middle Georgia Historical Society was initially chartered in 1964. Among its many accomplishments was a thorough professional survey of Macon's historic architecture. That 1970 survey formed the basis of a 1972 handbook, *A Guide to Macon's Architectural and Historical Heritage*. The Society also initiated the Middle Georgia Archives, a repository for important written materials, photographs, and artifacts significant in local history. For many years the society conducted semiannual rambles in historic Rose Hill Cemetery and used the proceeds for cemetery maintenance and restoration. These activities were turned over to the Rose Hill Cemetery Foundation by Historic Macon Foundation. Educational programs of the Middle Georgia Historical Society included presentations to schools to teach about local history and architecture and an oral history program to record the memories of long-term Macon residents for posterity.

In 1973, the Society acquired the 1840 cottage at 935 High Street that was the birthplace of noted poet, Sidney Lanier. The headquarters for the Society were housed in the upper level of the cottage, and the downstairs rooms were restored to serve as a museum open to the public and as a rental facility.

Recognizing that buying and selling property and carrying out actual restoration were beyond its scope, the Middle Georgia Historical Society joined forces with the Intown Macon Neighborhood Association in 1975 to create the Macon Heritage Foundation. The mission of the new organization was to save endangered historic buildings.

The Foundation saved literally hundreds of structures that otherwise would have been lost or destroyed. A "revolving fund" was used to buy or option properties, which were then rehabilitated or sold to other entities to complete the restoration. Each building's deed carries restrictive covenants to preserve the structure's historic appearance. Memberships, donations, grants, fundraisers, and partnerships were used to secure resources to accomplish the Foundation's mission.

In 1994, the Foundation embarked on a new scale of project, "Neighborhood Revitalization." Working in partnership with the National Trust for Historic Preservation, Mercer University, and

Sidney Lanier Cottage House Museum, childhood home of poet, musician, and soldier Sidney Clopton Lanier, was built around 1840.

private foundations, the Macon Heritage Foundation launched an ambitious endeavor to rescue the deteriorated Huguenin Heights neighborhood in the historic Tatnall Square Park area of Macon. Within just a few years, the neighborhood was transformed and, flushed with success, the Macon Heritage Foundation turned its attention and efforts to the Tatnall Square Heights neighborhood, where another transformation has been completed under the leadership of what is now Historic Macon Foundation. For its work in Tatnall Square Heights, Historic Macon was honored by the Georgia Trust for Historic Preservation in 2004 as the organization that had contributed the most to preservation in the state of Georgia in 2003. In addition to its real estate activities, the Macon Heritage Foundation served as an agency to provide numerous educational opportunities that focused on historic preservation by sponsoring tours, trips, lectures, and publications. The Foundation was also an advocate for Macon's eleven historic districts and a resource for experts in the restoration of historic buildings. The Macon Heritage Foundation won state, regional, and national awards for its efforts.

Committed strongly to the concept of "unity for the good of the community," the two founding organizations joined together in 2003 to become Historic Macon Foundation. The purpose of Historic Macon Foundation is to educate the greater Macon community about its history and historic preservation; preserve and restore historic buildings, sites and neighborhoods; and maintain and promote the Sidney Lanier Cottage.

Historic Macon Foundation sponsors lectures and tours and publishes books and calendars centered on Macon history. The foundation has two revolving funds. One fund continues to support the neighborhood revitalization work of Historic Macon, currently centered in the Beall's Hill neighborhood. The second revolving fund supports restoration projects that are not focused on neighborhoods, the last project being the purchase and stabilization of the Telephone Exchange Building, a significant downtown structure threatened with demolition by neglect. Historic Macon continues to operate the Sidney Lanier Cottage as a House Museum and rental facility. At the Sidney Lanier Cottage daily tours are given to tourists, residents, and school groups. Yearly over three thousand people, including hundreds of school children visit the Cottage. Publications and programs specifically geared toward Sidney Lanier, including monthly "Sidney's Salons" that feature both the works of Lanier and of local writers and musicians are offered at the Cottage. The monthly salons bring the literary and musical spirit of Sidney Lanier to Macon residents. Historic Macon also sponsors special events at the Cottage for Christmas and for the Cherry Blossom Festival.

Historic Macon is committed to continuing the legacies of its two parent organizations, while creating new opportunities to preserve and enhance the history and heritage of Macon.

The Historic Macon Foundation is located at 1083 Washington Avenue, Macon, Georgia, 31201. For more information about Historic Macon, call 478-742-5084, or visit the Web site at www.historicmacon.org.

❖

1083 Washington Avenue, the newly renovated headquarters of the Historic Macon Foundation. In the early 1900s this building reportedly was the first grocery store in Macon to let patrons pick out their own groceries.

Fore(In)Sight Foundation

Above: The late Dr. Bernard C. Murdock, Fore(In)Sight founder.

Below: Dr. Sandra C. Lewis, present president of Fore(In)Sight.

The Fore(In)Sight Foundation was founded in 1991 and has established itself as one of Macon's more proactive organizations, promoting the well-being of the community and with historical significance.

The principal founders of the Foundation are the late Dr. Bernard C. Murdoch, Emeritus Psychology Professor of Wesleyan College and prominent local psychologist and current Foundation President, Dr. Sandra Combs Lewis. Dr. Murdoch was Chairman of the Psychology Department, Chairman of the Behavioral Sciences Division, and Director of Testing at Wesleyan. He received a bachelor's degree from Appalachian State Teachers' College, Master's degrees from the University of Cincinnati and New York University, and his PhD from Duke University. Dr. Lewis, a Wesleyan College graduate, received Master's Degrees from Mercer University and Georgia State University, and her Ph.D. from the University of Georgia. She has been a part-time instructor in the Wesleyan Psychology Department and has served as the President of the Macon Wesleyan Alumnae Association.

The Foundation has a strong connection with Wesleyan College, and it strongly supports the Wesleyan community service mission and commitment to life-long learning.

"The Foundation's work is to present cognitive 'tools' that can enable persons to see the world not only differently but also more clearly. Where solutions are not apparent, we believe that at least the problems are clearer," Dr. Lewis commented.

In its mission statement Fore(In)Sight states that its primary purpose "is to provide a variety of communications that are intended to increase the happiness and well-being of individuals and our society in which they function." Elaborating further, the statement says that these communications are specifically directed at enabling each person to understand his/her basic potentials, as related to pertinent environmental factors, and the optimal education, vocations, marriage, morality beliefs, and use of time relevant to these potentials. To this end, the Foundation conveys ideas designed to reduce "preventable pain, suffering, and death" in the world, particularly that which is due to nonphysical causes that are referred to as being "behavioral." Fore(In)Sight perceives the production of positive behavior and the prevention of negative behavior to be intimately related, in that these involve behaviors, particularly behaviors that are due to nonphysical causes.

The Foundation's communications consist of four books to date with one more in process, monthly newsletters, a website, and individualized correspondence with associates. Seminars are held monthly along with occasional social suppers that highlight Fore(In)Sight concerns in after-dinner conversation. Volunteers, including the officers, do all the work.

The books produced include a basic reference entitled *Love and Problems of Living* and follow-up books of application of Behavioral Dynamics Principles in *God* and *Positive Christianity*, *Psychology for Life*, and *A Revolutionary View of EDUCATION AND TEACHING for the Third Millennium*. The newsletters are entitled *TRUTH SEEKERS* to show that the Foundation seeks the real truth about the complex behavioral issues with which it deals.

The Fore(In)Sight Foundation is relatively new, but it provides a unique and significant contribution to the dynamic history of Macon.

The Fore(In)Sight Foundation is located at 4976 Oxford Road, Macon, Georgia 31210-3059 and on the Internet at www.foreinsight.org.

1842 INN

When Nazario Filipponi and Edmund Olson took over Macon's venerable 1842 Inn eight years ago they inherited not only one of the nation's finest examples of an antebellum Greek Revival mansion, but also a part of the city's history that has included some of its leading citizens.

The Inn was built by prominent citizen John Gresham and went through many incarnations before becoming an award winning inn, which *Southern Home* magazine said, "…blends the amenities of a grand hotel with the ambiance of a country inn with classic Southern hospitality in grand antebellum style". The Inn boasts two period houses, the Main House (1842) and the Guest House (1902).

It was about 1900 when another prominent Macon family, the B.F. Adams, purchased the house and made significant changes. The original front porch in 1842 had only six columns and the Adams added side porches and added six more columns on each side. Today the Inn has eighteen columns giving it a look much like *Gone with the Wind*'s Tara.

The Inn, which now has about eighteen full and part-time employees was purchased by Olson and Filipponi in 1999 and is considered not only one of Macon's historical gems, but an important part of community and economic development in the city, including involvement with the Otis Redding Foundation and the Kevin Brown Celebrity Golf Tournament on behalf of the Macon Rescue Mission.

It has been designated by *Southern Living* magazine as one of the top ten Inns in the South. Future plans include additional guest rooms.

The Inn, which sits on 1.75 acres, now comprises nineteen guest rooms, hospitality parlors, service facilities, and a courtyard and porches for entertaining, and the Inn can accommodate approximately 150 guests for special events. It has attained a Four Diamond Award from the American Automobile Association of America and a Four Star Award from the Mobile Travel Association.

1842 is open year-round and is a member of some of the nation's top professional organizations, including Select Registry and Professional Association of Innkeepers' International.

Wesleyan College

Above: The warm and friendly atmosphere and small classes are conducive to developing critical thinking and leadership skills.

Below: The scenic and historic Wesleyan campus is the setting for women's education, which strives for excellence, is grounded in faith, and engaged in service to the world.

In 1836, Wesleyan College's founders dared dream that women could benefit from a rigorous study of liberal arts and deserved the same academic credentials as men, chartering the world's first college specifically for that purpose. History has proven them right–now, 170 years later, the private four-year liberal arts college continues to be a pioneer in higher education.

Consistently named to the "Princeton Review's Best 361 Colleges in America" as well as *U.S. News and World Report*'s annual listing of "America's Best Colleges," Wesleyan enjoys a reputation as one of the nation's premier educational institutions for women.

Wesleyan offers a distinctive, demanding, and relevant liberal arts academic program. Students from across the United States and twenty-three countries value the academic rigor and close ties offered by a ten to one student-teacher ratio, crediting both for their preparation to pursue graduate studies as well as their postgraduate successes in law, medicine, and other fields. Beyond the academic, Wesleyan offers a thriving residence life program, NCAA Division III athletics, championship IHSA equestrian program, and volunteer opportunities through its Lane Center for Community Engagement and Service.

Wesleyan students come from the four corners of the world to experience academic excellence and a rich history of sisterhood. Wesleyan is consistently cited nationally for its diversity and quality curriculum, and is among the most affordable private colleges in the nation.

"National studies continue to surface which validate what we at Wesleyan College see every day, particularly in the areas of engaged leadership and academic excellence in fields of math and science. These studies are another example of the increasing amount of research showing the advantages of single gender education," said Wesleyan President Ruth Knox. "What we have known intuitively and anecdotally since 1836 is now supported by a growing mound of empirical evidence. Women simply achieve more and learn more effectively at a women's college."

The school offers undergraduate degrees in thirty-five majors and twenty-nine minors including self-designed majors and interdisciplinary programs, as well as eight pre-professional programs including seminary, engineering, medicine, and law. A $12.5 million science center, added in 2007, enhanced the College's offerings further. Master of Arts degrees in education and an accelerated Executive Master of Business Administration program enroll both men and women. Wesleyan also offers a dual-degree program in engineering with the Georgia Institute of Technology in Atlanta; Auburn University in Auburn, Alabama; and Mercer University in Macon.

For additional information on Wesleyan College, visit www.wesleyancollege.edu on the Internet.

MACON-BIBB COUNTY TRANSIT AUTHORITY

City bus service became the dominate mode of public transportation in 1938 when the Georgia Power Company changed over from rail lines to bus service. Later the Transit System was owned by a private individual, Emmett Barnes III, and was known as the Bibb Transit Company. June Steraman, the only director who worked under the private ownership, continued as director when Bibb Transit became the Macon-Bibb County Transit Authority. Steraman was one of the longest serving members when she retired in 1995.

The City of Macon purchased Transit from Barnes in 1973, and the twenty-six year-old Macon-Bibb County Transit Authority was formed in 1980 by an act of the Georgia legislature. In 1981 the Authority began working toward the goal of its vision statement to "become a nationally recognized public transportation system."

Joseph McElroy, who worked for the system for thirty-one years and served as director the last part of those years, retired in late 2005 and leaves a legacy of steady progress with BTS and MTA. When he retired it was announced that current General Manager and CEO Carl Jackson would take over.

Jackson, who was serving as general manager of a bus rapid transit project in Ontario, Canada, when he was selected to become head of MTA after a nationwide search, has put several new initiatives on the agenda, including "working with stakeholders, elected officials, and the community on transit solutions that meet or exceed the transportation needs of the community."

The Transit Authority's Board is made up of individuals appointed by the Macon Mayor and the Board of Bibb County Commissioners, Mayor C. Jack Ellis and Commission Chairman Charles Ward Bishop, respectively. Presently serving on the Board are Tom Hudson, chairman; S. Craig Ross, vice chairman; Morris Cohen, secretary, and Board members Chuck Howard, Anderson Stroud, Jr., Nettie Thomas, and Deborah White.

Commenting on the future of the Transit Authority, General Manager Jackson stated, "MTA continues to commit resources to newer, more environmentally friendly buses to attract riders out of cars by improving the reliability of our current service."

❖

Above: Bibb Transit Company in the mid-twentieth century.

Below: The original terminal station built in 1916. It is the current location of the Macon-Bibb County Transit Authority at 200 Cherry Street in Macon.

Sharing the Heritage ✦ 89

JONES, CORK & MILLER, LLP

In 1872, only forty years after Macon was chartered, two remarkable lawyers from Jones County moved to Macon and formed a partnership known as Hardeman and Blount. Their law firm continues today, practicing under its current name, Jones, Cork & Miller, LLP.

The founders were outstanding lawyers and citizens. Both were true "Colonels" having achieved that rank in Georgia Battalions during the recent war. Isaac Hardeman, a Gettysburg survivor, served as a state senator, a Judge of the Ocmulgee Judicial Circuit and a prosecutor, a lifelong Sunday school superintendent at Mulberry and Vineville Methodist Churches, a trustee of Wesleyan College and a trustee of what is now the Methodist Home for Children and Youth. Hardeman Avenue is named for him as was the Hardeman Building (now Lawrence Mayer Florist) where the firm's offices were located for some years.

His partner, James H. Blount, was also an outstanding lawyer and public servant. He served twenty years in the U.S. House, was Speaker Pro Tem, and after retirement served as Special Commissioner to the Hawaiian Islands for President Cleveland and as Judge of the U. S. District Court for the Philippines.

Some other early partners who left their names on Macon are Buford Davis ("Buford Place"), Merrel P. Callaway ("Callaway Drive") and Orville A. Park, a noted Georgia legal scholar and Mercer law professor.

The names in the firm today honor our Jones family of attorneys, Bruce C., C. Baxter and George S. Jones and, today, Frank C. Jones, all descendants of Isaac Hardeman, and Charles M. Cork, a brilliant tax attorney, and Wallace Miller, Jr., third generation Macon trial lawyer.

The lawyers of Jones, Cork & Miller are proud to have played an important role in Macon's legal, business, civic and religious history for the past 135 years.

Jones, Cork & Miller is located at 435 Second Street in the SunTrust Bank Building on the fifth floor and on the Internet at www.jonescork.com.

Above: Founder Isaac Hardeman, Gettysburg survivor and state senator.

Right: Founder James H. Blount, outstanding lawyer and public servant.

GEICO

The Macon Regional Office of GEICO, which since 1996 has been a wholly owned subsidiary of Warren Buffett's Berkshire Hathaway, opened in 1974, and since that time has been an integral and important part of the company and the city.

GEICO started with a small twenty-two associate office in downtown Macon in June 1973. That same month then Governor and former President Jimmy Carter attended groundbreaking ceremonies for a new 245,500 square foot state-of-the-art building which would open with 750 employees and quickly expand to more than 1,000 middle Georgians by the end of the year. Ross Pierce was named as Macon's first Regional Vice President.

After twenty-four years of unprecedented growth, plans for a second GEICO office building in Macon were studied, and in 1998 the Macon-Bibb Industrial Authority pledged 29.5 acres for the project.

By 1998 rapid growth of the company's business set in motion plans for a second office building. Corporate management gave the green light for a new office building of 300,000 square feet adjacent to the existing property. A year later the legendary Buffett and state dignitaries, including then Congressman and now Senator Saxby Chambliss, were on hand for the grand opening of the new facility.

Today GEICO's two Macon buildings are home to more than 3,300 associates with an annual payroll of approximately $122 million. Regional Vice President John Izzo has responsibility for Southeast and Centralized Services Operations in the Macon 2 Facility, while Regional Vice President Mary Zarcone is in charge of the Midwest Profit Center House in the Macon 1 Facility.

Government Employees Insurance Company's (GEICO) history began in 1936 in Fort Worth, Texas, when Leo and Lillian Goodwin took a calculated risk to start up what has become one of the most successful and highly respected companies in the nation.

Leo hammered out the basic business plan for GEICO during his early career days in Texas. He believed that if he lowered costs in the company by marketing directly to carefully targeted customer groups, he would be able to pass along lower premiums and still earn a profit. He was right. The business began its upward climb, and in 1936 Goodwin established GEICO operations in Washington, D.C.

Lillian worked alongside her husband to launch the company and took an active role in virtually all aspects of the early operation. Lillian, a bookkeeper by profession, took on the accounting tasks but also worked to underwrite policies, set rates, issue policies, and market auto insurance to GEICO's target customers, federal employees and the top three grades of noncommissioned military officers. By the end of 1936 there were 3,700 GEICO policies in force and a total staff of twelve people.

The company grew steadily through the next six decades. Buffett bought his first stock in the 1950s. With the company rated a fiscally superior organization, Buffet made his second purchase of GEICO stock in 1976, reported to total one million shares. It was in 1995 that he made a bid for its remaining shares of the company, making GEICO a subsidiary of one of the most profitable organizations in the nation.

The Macon office has consistently grown over the past thirty-four years. GEICO is the nation's fastest growing auto insurance company. Due to the dedication, performance, and hard work of its associates, the Macon Regional Office has been selected for additional responsibilities over the years.

GEICO contributes in excess of $100,000,000 to the middle Georgia economy in terms of salary dollars (pre-tax). In addition, it also contributes hundreds of thousands of dollars and hundreds of hours of "person power" to local charitable organizations through its philanthropic activities and participation.

Commenting on the history of the Macon Regional Office, Izzo said, "The biggest change has been how we communicate with our policyholders. When we began operations here in 1973, we received all requests by mail or by phones and did most of our processing by passing paper forms around the office. We now receive the majority of applications for new policies, as well as a large portion of our policy changes, on the Internet, and the majority of our processing is now electronic. This has given our customer quicker service and has made us become even more efficient."

Truan Sales Inc.

Truan Sales Inc. is a leading manufacturer's representative of sewer pipe and fittings in the Southeast.

Andy Truan, founder and owner, has a nostalgic link to Macon, through his father, Joseph D. Truan, who was a B-24 pilot in WWII. Andy can recall how his Aunt "Lib" talked of staying at Macon's Historic Dempsey Hotel and would watch from her hotel window to see her brother march down Cherry Street. Andy's father, "Joe D" did his training at what is presently known as the Lewis B. Wilson Airport in Macon.

David A. "Andy" Truan is a 1967 graduate of Belmont University, Nashville, Tennessee. He worked in various capacities with different companies in the plastics industry but attributes his ten year tenure with the family owned business, Tridyn Industries, North Carolina as being invaluable experience in the PVC pipe and fittings. He went to work with the Dutch company DYKA as vice president of the PVC pipe division and established the plant that is now known as Diamond Plastics Inc. just south of Macon.

Truan Sales Inc. was incorporated in 1982 and has become recognized at the leading manufacturer's representative of PVC pipe and fittings in the Southeast. For the past two years, Truan Sales had been the top sales producer of its main line of products in the United States. A new 30,000 square foot warehouse was added to the existing 26,000 square foot warehouse/office. Consequently, Truan Sales expects even more growth in the future with the expanded space.

In 1984, Andy formed a second company, Pond Dam Piping, Ltd to sell various piping systems in the aquaculture and recreational pond market. Andy designed systems completely from PVC pipe and fittings which eliminated the expensive corrosion drawback to corrugated metal systems in use at that time.

Both companies benefit from a tight-knit, dedicated staff of sixteen employees. The employees strive to give the customer efficient, courteous service with each and every order placed.

Please visit Truan Sales Inc. on the Internet at www.truansales.com or you can visit www.ponddampiping.com.

❖

Andy Truan.

CARLYLE PLACE

The mission of Carlyle Place is to attain the highest possible quality of life for the residents who live there. Developed in 1996, as part of the Medical Center of Central Georgia's commitment to providing comprehensive healthcare across all sectors of the population, Carlyle Place opened its doors in 2001 as Macon's first and only Continuing Care Retirement Community specifically designed for people over the age of sixty-two. Fitness, independence, and healthcare, if needed, are hallmarks of this lovely community.

Located near the intersection of Bass and Foster Roads in the northwest corner of Macon, the beautifully landscaped fifty-five acre campus provides an unsurpassed environment. The community combines spacious independent apartment and garden homes, a maintenance free lifestyle with quality services, wellness, preventive health and a comprehensive Health Center, which includes assisted living, memory care and skilled nursing.

Carlyle Place focuses on finding and maintaining the optimal balance among the physical, spiritual, and emotional components of a "wellness lifestyle." Residents are freed from the responsibilities and burdens of home maintenance… free to focus on gratifying activities…free to explore new hobbies, business opportunities, travel destinations, sports, friendships and more. Whether it is discovering a hidden artistic talent, learning to e-mail, or fulfilling cultural interests through seminars, movies and travel, Carlyle Place offers a variety of options to enhance independence and wellness.

To help maintain an active lifestyle and good health, residents enjoy laps in the indoor pool, a relaxing long soak in the whirlpool spa or a healthy workout in the fitness rooms.

Residents also enjoy a variety of dining venues with a comfortable, convenient atmosphere to socialize with friends. Other amenities such as an on-site bank, a post office, a business center, a Hair and Nail Salon, and a gift shop…all of which paints a picture of daily convenience.

With close to 200 employees, the entire staff is dedicated to quality resident services and to creating opportunities for continued learning, growth, health, independence, serenity, camaraderie, comfort, and security.

Above: The Main Building of Carlyle Place.
COURTESY OF CHARLIE PETTIS, RESIDENT.

Below: East Campus.
COURTESY OF CHARLIE PETTIS, RESIDENT.

Macon Sewing Center

"Quality is what I look for," exclaimed Marilyn Sheldon, longtime owner of the Macon Sewing Center when she was asked to describe the essence of her approach to business. "Since 1975 the Sewing Center has been committed to service and selection with quality products at the best competitive price that can possibly be offered."

The Macon Sewing Center offers a complete line of high-end products, including not only sewing machines, but embroidery machines, combination sewing-embroidery machines, and sergers, plus fabrics and notions, which include, Marilyn believes, "probably the largest selection of buttons of any fabric store in the state."

The Sewing Center's brand product is the popular Baby Lock sewing machine and sergers made in Japan. Macon Sewing Center is one of the few sewing centers to offer instruction classes with every machine purchased, with emphasis on one-on-one instruction and guaranteed follow-up service.

When Marilyn bought the Sewing Center from her friend Ralph Smith in 1988, she owned her own business, "Windows and More," a home decorating business where her specialty was making draperies and home items. Smith, who founded the business in 1975, had continually urged her to buy the Center because he felt she would be a good manager and take good care of his customers. "I really didn't know that much about sewing machines," she said. But that very quickly changed, and with the help of her husband, George, who does repairs on the Center's machines, she has built a business with a loyal and steadily growing base with a long list of repeat customers, fulfilling Smith's prophecy that she "would be good at it."

In 2003 a major fire destroyed the business, but in only three weeks the Sewing Center was back in business down the street at 3076 Riverside Drive.

Active in the local Macon business community for years, Marilyn has served as president of the Greater Macon Women's Business Owners, and in 1999 was named Women's Business Owner of the Year.

Top: Marilyn Sheldon, owner of Macon Sewing Center in Macon, Georgia.

Bottom, Left: Present store location 2007.

Bottom, Right: Original store location 1975.

HAYS SERVICE, LLC

Hays Service, LLC is the outgrowth of the Hays Heating and Plumbing Company founded shortly after WWII in 1945 by Macon business and civic leader, Charles G. Hays, Sr. His vision was to start a business that could be passed on to his children and grandchildren, and today the third generation of the Hays' family, Cal Hays, Jr., carries on the family tradition.

Hays Service is a franchise operation of the LINC Service Network. The LINC Network is an organization of over 130 national and regional contractors headquartered in Pittsburg, Pennsylvania. The company was started by Cal Hays, Jr. in 1999. It was his father, Jim Hays, son of patriarch Charles Hays, Sr., who advanced the technology in the business to include air conditioning, and the name was changed to Hays Mechanical Contractors in the 1970s.

When Cal, Jr. graduated from Georgia Tech in 1977, just like his father had done before him, he joined the company and expanded services which prompted changing the name of the business to The Hays Corporation of Georgia.

It was in 1999 when Cal, Jr. decided to organize a company to take over the services and maintenance business, which was operating as a separate division of the Hays Corporation. The new company is Hays Service, LLC.

"Our focus has changed from construction to service, but increasing the value to our customers is always our goal," Cal, Jr. commented. "Our business plan is assisted by the LINC Group and is virtually unlimited in opportunities. With rising energy costs and the 'Green' movement initiatives, our unique business of guaranteeing peak efficiency of heating and air conditioning equipment comes quickly to the forefront of alert financial managers."

Among the company's clients of more than thirty years are Macon's YKK, (USA), Wesleyan College and many other local and regional businesses.

The Hays family and company officials have over the years been leaders in community and civic affairs. Rotary, Chambers of Commerce, and United Way are among the many organizations in which they participate.

Top, Left: Founder Charles G. Hays, Sr.

Top, Right: Father and son, Jim and Cal, Jr.

Macon Convention & Visitors Bureau

The Macon-Bibb Convention & Visitors Bureau began in 1978 as an outgrowth of the Greater Macon Chamber of Commerce and was incorporated as an independent destination marketing organization in 1982. The next year Janice Marshall joined the CVB, and was named executive director in 1986, later becoming president and CEO. Under her leadership the Bureau has won many awards, including recognition four times as the best in the tourism industry's Southeast region.

As the CVB grew over time, its offices and downtown visitors center moved to larger facilities: the Macon Coliseum from 1980-1990, and the Macon Terminal Station from 1990-2007.

Macon's most visible music legend, Little Richard, signed on as the CVB's official goodwill ambassador for tourism in 2000 with the unveiling of Macon's new branding as the Song & Soul of the South, lending his image, and even video and voice to the Bureau's marketing efforts at no cost.

With the opening in 2007 of a new multipurpose visitors center, training and resource center and marketing office, the CVB reached a milestone in its history, which will greatly enhance its ability to carry out its mission to help meet the economic needs of Macon, Middle Georgia, and a large portion of rural Georgia.

Housed in the former Trailways Bus station in historic downtown, the new facility was designated as "The Best of the Best" in Georgia by Governor Sonny Purdue and was recognized by Historic Macon with an Adaptive Re-Use Award in 2007. Easily accessible from Interstate 16, the new center is within walking distance of many key downtown attractions, such as the Georgia Sports Hall of Fame, the Georgia Music Hall of Fame, the $15 million future home of the Tubman African-American Museum, and Macon's shopping, dining, arts and entertainment district.

As a tourism revenue generator, the CVB brings people from outside the area into Macon and the surrounding region to infuse revenue into the economy and support job retention and growth.

Additional information may be found on the Internet at www.visitmacon.org.

Above: The new Downtown Macon Visitors Center and CVB offices in 2007.

Below: Little Richard and crew visit the CVB offices in 2006.

PARKS & ROBERTS TAX SERVICE

Parks & Roberts Tax Service is a subsidiary of J. Parks and Co., Inc. with corporate offices located at 3640 Eisenhower Parkway, Suite 120 in Macon, Georgia. J. Parks, Inc., is a privately held company that is completely owned by its stockholders and founded by Jack Parks, Sr.

Since its inception in the mid-eighties, J. Parks Co., Inc., has seen tremendous growth in the tax and financial field. Parks & Roberts Tax Service was added under the umbrella of J. Parks, Inc., in January 1987 when Jack Parks and Cleo Roberts, who were previous employed by the tax preparation firm of H&R Block, combined their resources and talents to form one of Georgia's best and most respected tax preparation businesses in the region. Parks & Roberts offers a complete line of federal and state income tax preparations as well as payroll services, bookkeeping, filing tax reports, tax training school, and notary service.

Parks & Roberts Tax Service currently has a staff of twenty, which includes full and part time employees and has customers throughout the United States.

Parks & Roberts have clients in every region of the country and its business continues to strive and grow throughout the nation. This growth can be attributed to the respect and high regards given it by its many clients who continually and wholeheartedly endorse and recommend our services to others. In order to stay in step with the demands of growth and better serve our clients, Parks and Roberts found it necessary to open offices in the downtown east area of Macon and most recently opened offices in Warner Robins and the Metro Atlanta area. As the needs arise and growth continues Parks & Roberts Tax Service will look courageously to the future by maintaining reliable service, a high degree of customer satisfaction, and staying at the summit of changes.

Supporting the Tubman African American Museum and Bibb County Public Schools are just a couple examples of how Parks & Roberts Tax Service is involved in the community in which they work and live.

Parks & Roberts Tax Service has received many compliments throughout the years including:
- Parks and Roberts' fifty years experience with taxes;
- Family-oriented office;
- Friendly and helpful staff; and
- Honesty and integrity.

With the vision and business skills of its founders, continued support from its stockholders and a very competent staff, Parks & Roberts Tax Service will continue to be the very best and most successful tax preparation business in the universe.

Broadway Lofts

The recent history of Broadway Lofts is a story of one man's effort against long odds to save a Macon historical architectural gem and turn it into a place where local residents could find upscale loft living and shopping.

The historic Happ Brothers Manufacturing building is at the corner of Macon's Broadway and Pine in the railroad district and was built in 1916 to produce Happ overalls. The company was the city's largest downtown employer for sixty years.

When Vern McCarty, president of McCarty Property Group of Atlanta, happened upon the Happ building in 1999, it was doomed for demolition. The reason it caught his eye was because it was similar to industrial buildings in Atlanta, which MPG had converted to residential and business lofts.

Plans were underway to tear down the building and sell its vintage bricks, which at the time were deemed more valuable than the real estate. Acting quickly, McCarty made an offer for the 120,000 square foot edifice, and with the backing of the Medical Center of Central Georgia, which held title to the building and had an interest in the revitalization of downtown Macon, he was successful. The Center's commitment to downtown development was so strong it took less money from MPG than it would have gained by selling the bricks.

"So how did history win out over dollars?" McCarty asks rhetorically, "Because the Medical Center believed in the future of historic downtown. Today, Broadway Lofts is worth much more than the bricks which formed its walls."

The complex is a live-work environment where many residents walk to work or to downtown restaurants, and since it is zoned commercial it is home to several businesses.

Coincidentally, the largest single bloc of residents is from the Macon medical community. Broadway Lofts has ninety-one loft apartments, plus six store front retail/office lofts.

Commenting on the project McCarty said, "Broadway Lofts represents the best America has to offer and is a triumph of the human spirit, at times against long odds."

A. T. Long & Son Painting

A.T. Long & Son Painting has a long history and family tradition of care and craftsmanship in a wide variety of genres, including residential, commercial, industrial, and more recently, historical work.

A.T. Long, who founded the company in 1942 before serving in the Navy during WWII, began his long career in the business in the 1930s when he worked with family members in a Thomaston painting company. Just prior to the war, A.T. took over work for the company in Bibb and Houston Counties. When he returned to Macon after the war he went back to work under his own company banner.

In 1953 while still in high school, A.T.'s son, Tony, began working in the business. After graduating from high school, he worked part time while attending Mercer University, majoring in economics and math. Upon graduating in 1964, he entered the business full time.

From the beginning the Long family took great pride in their craft, gaining a reputation for quality work, no matter the type job. In the early years, jobs consisted primarily of residential, commercial and industrial work.

In the 1970s, Tony was asked to paint one of the pre Civil War churches in historic Madison, which led to jobs painting some of that city's historic homes. Because of this work the company has become known for the quality of its painting and finishing work for historic buildings. It is one of the most important aspects of A.T. Long's business. As examples, some of the company's recent projects have included the old Governor's mansion in Milledgeville, and in Macon a number of historic homes and churches, the Hay House, the Grand Opera House, and the Cox Capitol theater.

In the late 1970s and early 1980s, Tony worked with the late Macon music legend, Phil Walden, saving and renovating homes in the in-town district of Macon. His most recent venture is renovating old buildings in downtown Macon, continuing the company's more than six decade involvement in the growth and progress of Macon and middle Georgia.

Above: Tony Long teaching daughter, Kate at the age of nine, how to apply sizing for gold leaf in St. Joseph's Church.

PHOTOGRAPH COURTESY OF MARYANN BATES.

Below: A.T. Long, 1917-1999.

Sharing the Heritage ✦ 99

Pilot International

When women received the right to vote in 1921, Macon's Elizabeth Leonard used this momentous occasion as a catalyst to create a women's organization, which would provide meaningful community services in communities around the world. She immediately met with six of her friends and formed Pilot International.

Lucy B. Allen was chosen the first president of the new club which was named Pilot after river boat pilots who were known to navigate a "true course." The first international convention was held in Macon the next year at the Dempsey Hotel. The organization's code of ethics, in use since 1926, was written by Alabama native Pearl Sparks.

From the charter of the first club in Macon, Pilot International grew to over 600 clubs in the 1980s and is now at approximately 500 clubs. In 1982, Pilot International created Anchor Clubs for youth. Membership today consists of approximately 12,000 Pilots and 10,000 Anchors.

One of the many international community projects for which Pilot International is noted occurred immediately after WWII when it rebuilt a French village, which was accidentally bombed by U.S. troops. Also following the war, Pilot International became the first women's service organization to sponsor Project HOPE on an international basis, completely redoing the pediatric ward of the hospital ship *USS HOPE*.

Pilot's signature focus is education and protection regarding brain injury and brain disorders. Grants and scholarships from Pilot International Foundation help fund many programs.

Pilot International's headquarters was first established in the Person's Building on Mulberry Street in Macon. A fire in the building destroyed most of the organization's records in 1959. Pilot International established a new headquarters in 1964 at 244 College Street. The organization began construction of a new headquarters building in 2006 at 102 Preston Court off of Old Forsyth Road in the Bass Road complex. This new facility will be able to provide additional services and will be an important step toward rejuvenating memberships and clubs worldwide. Dedication is scheduled for February 2008.

MACON CENTREPLEX

Though the Macon Centreplex name is just over a decade old, two of its three facilities are a huge part of Macon's rich history, and all three are catalysts for Macon's promising future.

Owned by the City of Macon, the Centreplex includes the Macon City Auditorium, the Macon Coliseum and the Edgar H. Wilson Convention Center, a trio of flexible facilities that make the Centreplex one of the largest entertainment and convention facilities in the southeast.

Built in 1925, the Auditorium is nestled in the heart of downtown. It is listed on the National Register of Historic Places and its copper dome is reported to be the largest in the world. The facility's 2,688-seat theatre has hosted many legendary and current performers to include Macon's own Otis Redding, Little Richard, and the Allman Brothers Band. In addition to concerts, this elegant facility is also a popular place for plays and conventions as well as banquets, wedding receptions and other private events.

Opened in 1968, the Coliseum was the first venue of its size and type in Georgia and has hosted full-house crowds for superstars such as Elvis Presley, Elton John, Cher, and Kenny Chesney. With more than 9,000 seats, the Coliseum is also popular for conventions, trade shows and sporting events as well as public ice-skating.

The Edgar H. Wilson Convention Center was opened for business in 1996. It combines with the Coliseum to offer more than 120,000 square feet of useable meeting and exhibit space all under one roof. The convention center features a 30,800 square foot exhibit hall, a sub-dividable ballroom, and eighteen other meeting and breakout rooms.

The complex hosts' nearly 2,000 events per year and offers clients one-stop shopping from full-service in-house catering to state-of-the-art audiovisual, event coordination and marketing services. It has been chosen a Prime Site Award winner for nine years running by the readers of *Facilities Magazine*–a major meetings and conventions publication.

For more information, please visit the website www.maconcentreplex.com or call 478-751-9154.

Above: Edgar H. Wilson Convention Center.

Below: Macon City Auditorium.

Mercer University

Mercer and Macon have had a strong relationship ever since the University moved to the city from Penfield, Georgia in 1871. As Macon has blossomed into an economic engine for Middle Georgia, Mercer has expanded its programs to meet the growing academic needs.

Founded in 1833, Mercer offered only a liberal arts education until 1873, when it added a School of Law. The school, later named for U.S. Senator Walter F. George, was a perfect fit for Macon, which had an active legal community and was home to state, district and federal courts. Over the decades, graduates included Congressman Carl Vinson, U.S. Attorney General Griffin B. Bell, former Georgia Secretary of State Cathy Cox, and U.S. District Judge William Augustus "Gus" Bootle.

In the 1970s, Mercer addressed a growing crisis—the need for physicians, especially in rural and medically underserved areas of Georgia. Macon leaders asked Mercer to establish a medical school and the University sought and received funding assistance from the state of Georgia. Mercer promised to help keep the physicians they educated in the state by accepting only Georgia residents into the program.

In the 1980s, Robins Air Force Base, the largest employer in Middle Georgia, needed more qualified engineers to ensure its continuing operations. The Base commander approached the University and, once again, Mercer answered the call. The first class of the School of Engineering enrolled in 1985. Today, Mercer is the number one provider of engineers to the Base.

The next need Mercer tackled was Georgia's call for educators. Its teacher education programs became the Tift College of Education. The college has the largest enrollment within the University, offering bachelors, masters, specialists and Ph.D. degrees, and is the largest teacher education program among Georgia's private institutions.

Mercer's community contributions are not limited to academics. Mercer University Press has published more than 1,200 books since 1979. The University manages the historic Grand Opera House, which hosts Broadway shows and is home to the Macon Symphony Orchestra.

Right: The R. Kirby Godsey Administration Building, which houses the Office of the President, was the first building constructed on Mercer University's Macon campus.

Below: The Princeton Review *selected Mercer University's Macon campus as one of the most beautiful campuses in the country.*

MEDICAL CENTER OF CENTRAL GEORGIA

Macon in the late 1890s was a bustling, rapidly growing community. Yet, it was missing something.

"Though it was still the days of horse-and-buggy doctors and hospitalization was still a new concept, a group of concerned citizens decided Macon really needed a facility to care for the sick and injured," CEO and President Don Faulk said, recounting his hospital's rich history. "And, on March 27, 1895, The Macon Hospital—now the Medical Center of Central Georgia—officially opened its doors."

Initially, the facility was located at 820 Pine Street and offered accommodations for just four private and sixteen ward patients. Atlanta physician Olin H. Weaver was recruited to organize the new hospital, and he and his staff of one nurse, two maids, two orderlies, one cook, and a nurse superintendent, served a blooming population of 22,000 residents.

Today, the Medical Center of Central Georgia (MCCG) is Georgia's second largest hospital. It is a 501(c) (3) private, not-for-profit corporation owned by the Macon-Bibb Hospital Authority and is a part of the Central Georgia Health System. It is a designated Level I Trauma Center and Magnet™ hospital for nursing and has approximately 5,000 employees and a medical staff of more than 500 physicians serving an estimated population of 750,000 in a 28-county area. The facility boasts more than 630 beds in medical-surgical, obstetric, pediatric, psychiatric, cardiac intensive care, neurology intensive care, pediatric intensive care, and cardiac surgery intensive care units.

Distinguished nationally for its excellence, MCCG is one of the premier teaching hospitals in America and serves as the primary teaching hospital for the Mercer University School of Medicine, providing residency programs for more than one hundred residents.

In addition to its award-winning in-patient services, MCCG also offers a broad range of community-based, outpatient diagnostic, primary and, urgent-care services, extensive home-health and hospice-care services, as well as comprehensive rehab services. The center strives to make excellence a daily standard.

The Medical Center of Central Georgia is located at 777 Hemlock Street in Macon. For more information, please call 478-633-1000 or visit www.mccg.org.

Coldwell Banker SSK

In 1975 with a card table, four chairs, and a single telephone, three Macon real estate brokers founded what has become Middle Georgia's leading residential real estate firm. Peter Solomon, Gene Kernaghan and the late Val Sheridan had the foresight to build a better mousetrap in the world of home buying and selling when they opened their business in a small office on Walnut Street in downtown Macon.

"The card table belonged to the agency and we had to take turns using the phone. Our goal even then was to dominate residential real estate in Macon and Bibb County. That was our hope and dream," according to Solomon.

The dream became a reality through the hard work, concern for clients and commitment to excellence over the past thirty years. As the company grew, the partners moved from the rented office in downtown Macon to a renovated A&P grocery store on Vineville Avenue in 1979. They added agents, increased listings and sales and quickly became known as the top-drawer real estate agency for the area.

"By 1981, we had become number one in Bibb County and Macon. Our vision grew beyond county lines to serve all of central Georgia and that's just what we've done," said Solomon. Throughout the 1980s and into the 1990s, the three partners applied their knowledge of the business and their standings in the community to build the firm, which now has 150 Realtors in four offices and a forty member administrative staff.

In 1996, two of the partners sold their interests in the company. David Green, Russell Lipford, Bert Witham and Steve Bullard acquired two-thirds of the company from Sheridan and Kernaghan. The firm also opened an office in Warner Robins that year as its first satellite location.

"Val decided to retire around his seventh-fifth birthday and Gene had a good opportunity to work in telecommunications services, so four great partners bought their shares of the business," Solomon said. "It began another chapter for us."

In 1997, Sheridan-Solomon-Kernaghan affiliated with Coldwell Banker, changing its name to Coldwell Banker SSK. It also began a strong expansion program, a vision Solomon had nurtured for several years.

"The technology and national identity that Coldwell Banker brings to the table has moved us forward," Solomon said. "The new partners share my philosophy and vision for expansion as well."

By 2000 the company had built a new building in Warner Robins. Two years later, the firm again expanded to Gray, setting up a full-service office east of Macon in Jones County.

In the fall of 2002, Coldwell Banker SSK moved into a brand new state-of-the-art sixteen-thousand-square-foot building on Bass Road, just a quarter mile west of I-75. It houses the company's corporate operations for all of Middle Georgia, as well as the Macon sales office. Training space, a conference area, smaller conference rooms and nearly fifty private offices give the company the most comprehensive facility in the area.

By 2004, rapid residential growth in central Georgia supported the need for another office, this time in Milledgeville in Baldwin County. It brought the total number of Coldwell Bank SSK offices to four.

With growth came a more formal corporate structure. Solomon serves the firm as CEO; Shirley Lewis, a successful real estate broker with the firm and a long-time international businesswoman was named president in 2005.

Today the company handles relocation services for many of the companies moving their offices to Middle Georgia. Through Coldwell Banker, it also has a mortgage division. The company expanded career opportunities in the area through the opening of Middle Georgia Academy of Real Estate, which offers creative, interesting and informative courses in support of state minded education programs for real estate licensure and continuing education for professional competency. Designation and certification programs are held year-round at the company's Bass Road offices.

"Coldwell Banker SSK is involved in one in every five residential real estate transactions in Middle Georgia," Solomon said. "It's happened through hard work and dedication of the people in our company. Our goal is to continue to concentrate on market share in this area, by being alert to the latest technology, taking good care of our employees and our customers and by being ready fro opportunity before it happens."

Corporate headquarters for Coldwell Banker SSK is located at 1501 Bass Road in Macon and on the Internet at www.coldwellbankerssk.com.

GEORGIA POWER

More than seventy years ago, Georgia Power's first president, Preston Arkwright, Sr., spoke the words that have guided generations of Georgia Power employees: "A citizen wherever we serve."

Georgia Power–the largest subsidiary of its parent Southern Company, one of the country's largest power generators–works with community leaders on a variety of initiatives to support education, enhance the local economy and protect the environment. It serves two-million customers statewide. Good citizenship begins with customer satisfaction, built on high reliable service and rates below the national average. In addition, energy conservation and green energy continues to be a priority for Georgia Power.

Locally, Thomas J. Wicker, region vice president, oversees the 233 employees and more than 167,000 customers in twenty-six counties in central Georgia. Georgia Power believes in having a presence in the communities it serves by providing nineteen business offices in the Macon, Milledgeville, Dublin, Perry and Vidalia areas to serve its customers.

Georgia Power demonstrates its continuing commitment to being an active presence in Macon and central Georgia by its involvement with significant community issues and concerns. Locally, Georgia Power employees serve on local boards and take leadership roles with the Chambers of Commerce that helps impact the economy.

To ensure safer air quality, Georgia Power has spent $1 billion on environment controls since 1990, and will spend an additional $3 billion over the next five years. Georgia Power also supports other environmental projects to preserve and protect precious natural resources from planting trees to taking a leadership role in carpooling and alternative fuels.

Georgia Power is located at 960 Key Street in Macon, Georgia. For more information, visit Georgia Power on the Internet at www.georgiapower.com.

Sponsors

1842 Inn	87
A. T. Long & Son Painting	99
Anderson, Walker & Reichert, LLP	72
Atlantic Southern Bank	66
Broadway Lofts	98
Carlyle Place	93
Coldwell Banker SSK	104
Fore(In)Sight Foundation	86
GEICO	91
Georgia Power	105
Hays Service, LLC	95
Historic Macon Foundation	84
Jean and Hall Florists	80
Jones, Cork & Miller, LLP	90
Macon Centreplex	101
Macon Convention & Visitors Bureau	96
Macon Sewing Center	94
Macon Water Authority	78
Macon-Bibb County Transit Authority	89
Medical Center of Central Georgia	103
Mercer University	102
Mount de Sales Academy	82
Nu-Way Weiners	70
Parks & Roberts Tax Service	97
Pilot International	100
River Edge Behavioral Health Center	76
Smith & Sons Foods	74
Truan Sales, Inc.	92
Wesleyan College	88

About the Author

James E. Barfield, Jr.

James Everett Barfield, Jr., represents the fifth generation of his family to live in Bibb County, Georgia. A retired history teacher, he holds degrees from the University of North Carolina at Chapel Hill, Mercer University and Georgia College and State University. He served as president (twice) of the Middle Georgia Historical Society and of the Macon Heritage Foundation, and as president of the Historic Macon Foundation, their successor. He was founding president of the Historic Rose Hill Cemetery Foundation and since 1990 has led tours through that historic cemetery. In 2004, he authored *Living Macon Style*, a book celebrating residential architecture in his hometown. He regularly contributes articles on architectural history, preservation, and antiques to Macon Magazine.

About the Cover

George Beattle (1919-1997) lived in Georgia the last half-century of his life and is buried in Macon's Rose Hill Cemetery. He studied art at the Cleveland Institute of Art before beginning his lifelong career as a painter. He taught art at the High Museum in Atlanta, at Georgia Tech, and at Georgia State University. In 1963 he painted the mural *A Historic View of Middle Georgia* to be installed in the main entryway of Macon's College Street U.S. Post Office. Permission to use portions of the mural was granted by the artist's family and by the U.S. Postal Service.

Photographs of the mural were taken by Walter G. Elliott. His photographs also appear on pages 53, 59 (lower), 60 (two photos), and 61.

The photograph of Judge Emory Speer on page 40 is courtesy of the Furman Smith Law Library of Mercer University.

All other photographs accompanying the history text are used by the generous cooperation and permission of the Middle Georgia Archives, Washington Memorial Library.

For more information about the following publications or about publishing your own book, please call Historical Publishing Network at 800-749-9790 or visit www.lammertinc.com.

Black Gold: The Story of Texas Oil & Gas

Historic Abilene: An Illustrated History

Historic Albuquerque: An Illustrated History

Historic Amarillo: An Illustrated History

Historic Anchorage: An Illustrated History

Historic Austin: An Illustrated History

Historic Baton Rouge: An Illustrated History

Historic Beaufort County: An Illustrated History

Historic Beaumont: An Illustrated History

Historic Bexar County: An Illustrated History

Historic Brazoria County: An Illustrated History

Historic Charlotte:
An Illustrated History of Charlotte and Mecklenburg County

Historic Cheyenne: A History of the Magic City

Historic Comal County: An Illustrated History

Historic Corpus Christi: An Illustrated History

Historic Denton County: An Illustrated History

Historic Edmond: An Illustrated History

Historic El Paso: An Illustrated History

Historic Erie County: An Illustrated History

Historic Fairbanks: An Illustrated History

Historic Gainesville & Hall County: An Illustrated History

Historic Gregg County: An Illustrated History

Historic Hampton Roads: Where America Began

Historic Henry County: An Illustrated History

Historic Houston: An Illustrated History

Historic Illinois: An Illustrated History

Historic Kern County:
An Illustrated History of Bakersfield and Kern County

Historic Lafayette:
An Illustrated History of Lafayette & Lafayette Parish

Historic Laredo:
An Illustrated History of Laredo & Webb County

Historic Louisiana: An Illustrated History

Historic Midland: An Illustrated History

Historic Montgomery County:
An Illustrated History of Montgomery County, Texas

Historic Ocala: The Story of Ocala & Marion County

Historic Oklahoma: An Illustrated History

Historic Oklahoma County: An Illustrated History

Historic Omaha:
An Illustrated History of Omaha and Douglas County

Historic Ouachita Parish: An Illustrated History

Historic Paris and Lamar County: An Illustrated History

Historic Pasadena: An Illustrated History

Historic Passaic County: An Illustrated History

Historic Philadelphia: An Illustrated History

Historic Prescott:
An Illustrated History of Prescott & Yavapai County

Historic Richardson: An Illustrated History

Historic Rio Grande Valley: An Illustrated History

Historic Scottsdale: A Life from the Land

Historic Shreveport-Bossier:
An Illustrated History of Shreveport & Bossier City

Historic South Carolina: An Illustrated History

Historic Smith County: An Illustrated History

Historic Texas: An Illustrated History

Historic Victoria: An Illustrated History

Historic Tulsa: An Illustrated History

Historic Williamson County: An Illustrated History

Historic Wilmington & The Lower Cape Fear:
An Illustrated History

Iron, Wood & Water: An Illustrated History of Lake Oswego

Miami's Historic Neighborhoods: A History of Community

Old Orange County Courthouse: A Centennial History

Plano: An Illustrated Chronicle

The New Frontier:
A Contemporary History of Fort Worth & Tarrant County

The San Gabriel Valley: A 21st Century Portrait

The Spirit of Collin County